Good Car Ma

Alan Hurst

Legacy Book Press LLC
Camanche, Iowa

To Charlie

Chapters

Chapter 1

Peggy and Ron

Their third child, Julie, was born mentally retarded. In the sixties they didn't call it autistic. They didn't call it special. They called it unfortunate. It was a challenge, but it wasn't a curse. It was what you signed up for. Peggy and her husband Ron had just had twins a year earlier, a boy and a girl. That should have been enough. Peggy was thirty-four and Ron was fifty. She had remained a single woman until the last minute, and he was a bachelor, retired from the navy and the war. When they met at a summer retreat in the scenic Rocky Mountains of Canada, they both knew it was their last chance to have a family. The couple immediately got married. Less than two years later, they already had three kids.

According to Freud, a woman carries a purse because it is an unconscious metaphor for her womb. Peggy's Volkswagen van carried her most important belongings. It was the vehicle that transported her offspring, like a mother kangaroo carries her kids from place to place, until they are old enough and strong enough to jump out into the world on their own. Julie wasn't able to do that. She would never talk or be able to take care of herself. Peggy knew it, and so did Ron. That was how it was. It was going to be a long journey, with a great reward.

Before he met Peggy, Ron had never needed to carry anything, except a duffel bag and his shaving kit. Whichever ship he was aboard was the only vessel he ever depended on. It housed him, fed him, clothed him, protected him, and guided him through treacherous seas and into safe harbors. Her Majesty had always called the shots, and for over three decades he had served her. Now he suddenly had no orders to follow. He was unmoored from his duties, directionless and free. Then he met Peggy—the woman who became the captain of his destiny. He followed her command and trusted her completely. He did so until the end of his life. He was in good hands, and he knew it.

In 1930, Ron had little choice but to join the navy. The Great Depression was already ravaging England, and there were few options for a young lad just out of school. His father had given him a simple choice: join the police or join the navy. He was sixteen. A friend of his father's was a constable at the local precinct. He invited the boy around for the day to see how he liked it. Young Ronny said being a policeman didn't much appeal to him, so that was that. He enlisted in the British merchant navy, left his home in Yorkshire, and immediately boarded a cargo ship out of Liverpool headed to South America. He didn't return to England for another two years. He was shipped off again. He went to every place you can go. Eventually, he circled the world three times. He made it through the war and finally to retirement.

On his first voyage, a schooner took him across the Atlantic to a distant port in the tropics. Everywhere there were kids running around like flies, tugging at his pant legs and begging for food or money. Young Ron and his sailor mates stumbled into a cafe that offered a little shade from the hot Brazilian sun. A man came out and asked them what they wanted to drink. They looked around, "Whatever those kids are having." The proprietor came back in a few minutes with their order. Ron said, "Hey! This is beer!" and the man said, "Yeah, you said you wanted what the kids are drinking." After Brazil they went to Argentina, then around Cape Horn, across the Pacific to India, then to the Middle East and up the Suez Canal, then all the way back around South Africa, and up the Ivory Coast.

That same year, Peggy was born in a busy hospital in New York City. Her mother was only fifteen. The young woman had run away from her family and was toiling away as a domestic servant in a workhouse for wayward girls. It was a miserable place, but there was little else for a girl in her shoes. The runaway met an Irish immigrant named Burns who was five years older. He got her pregnant. The young mother, either with or without the help of the child's father, made an effort to take care of her baby as best she could. She tried for a number of months, but it just became too hard. She had named the child Millicent. Millicent was strong and healthy, and hungry. Finally, one morning, her mother made the somber decision to give her infant up for adoption. She entered an orphanage in Brooklyn who took in the child, and immediately found a good home for her with a nice couple who had the means to raise her in those tough times. They were a childless couple in their thirties, who lived in nearby Hackettstown, New Jersey. The husband was a dairy salesman who had managed to remain gainfully employed despite the Depression. His wife Harriet had been unable to have children of her own. They brought home the baby girl and renamed her Margaret Louise. She was raised as an only child in a middle-class neighborhood. Later in school, she got the nickname, Peggy.

When Peggy got old enough, her parents told her that she had been adopted. As she eventually grew into an independent young woman, Peggy struggled with the circumstances of her birth. She obviously felt somewhat abandoned and confused. She wanted to know the truth; she wanted answers about her real parents. But Peggy's mother felt resentment about her curiosity, and she refused to divulge the details. "You should be grateful! You would be in the gutter if it weren't for your father and me!" In a spiteful rage, her mother opened the family safe and burned the records of Peggy's adoption, right in front of her. After that, they never talked about it again. Peggy didn't forget that unforgiveable incident. It caused a bitter rift between the mother and daughter that was never repaired. It was only years and years later, just before her death, that Peggy found out the true facts of her birth and was finally able to gain the peace and closure that had haunted her all her life.

Upon graduation from high school in 1948, Peggy left home for college. She was independent and ambitious. She wanted to travel far away and take on the world. She did just that. She earned a master's degree in home economics and set off for England. She was awarded a teaching scholarship at Stratford-upon-Avon, where she taught cooking and sewing at a British boarding school for half a dozen seasons. In the summers, she traveled extensively throughout Europe to France, Germany, Spain, Italy, Denmark, Belgium, and Switzerland. Her friends were all getting married, but Peggy wasn't ready to settle down yet. She returned to the States still restless and single. Her mother shamed her. "You're going to be an old maid." Within a few years, however, she met Ron and had children. After the twins were born, Peggy's mother warned her not to have a third child. "Quit while you're ahead," she said. Maybe it was for the satisfaction of proving her mother wrong. Anyway, it's not selfish to want to have more children.

After Julie was born, they noticed something was wrong. For several months, they thought she might be deaf. Once the diagnosis of her retardation had been confirmed, it only made things worse between Peggy and her mother. But it wasn't Julie's fault. You couldn't use her like that. You couldn't forsake an innocent and disabled child. She was the way she was. It wasn't about revenge or "I told you so." It had just happened, that's all, and for a reason which nobody understood or could ever solve. There were plenty of attempts to find doctors and do tests that might have provided some hope or offered a meaningful explanation. What was the point? They would never know why or how it had happened, and they eventually stopped asking. You can't look at it as a bad thing. You try to make life rewarding as best you can—not just for yourself.

Peggy had been on her own for a good time, making sure she got what she needed, and what she deserved. But now Peggy's life was not only about herself anymore; it was about her children and her husband. She held the family all together and took them with her. It was that Volkswagen van, strangely enough, which ended up being her greatest ally. It was a symbol and a vehicle of her fortitude and persistence, of conquering adversity, surviving, and thriving and never giving up. It was like a portable safety deposit box containing all the memories and adventures she collected along the way. It kept her family protected and together. She kept the car going and it kept her going. She carried us all, from one place to the next place, and to a better place after that. She plowed ahead without any regrets. She drove us to our destination. She left the sorrows and the tribulations of the past in the rearview mirror, and never looked back. For Peggy, it was personal. It was a job only she could have taken on; it was a life only she could have accomplished. She did it well and she completed the job. That is what this book is about.

Chapter 2

The Sportsmobile

In August of 1963, just eight weeks after they met, the couple got married at the local courthouse in Peggy's hometown of Hackett-stown, New Jersey. They traveled to England briefly to meet Ron's mum and sister, and then turned around and headed back to a new life in the States. From there, the newlyweds took their first road trip together. They bought an old Rambler station wagon and hit the road, traveling south of the border to San Miguel de Allende in central Mexico. San Miguel was a small cobble-stoned oasis snuggled deep in the mountains of Guanajuato. Diego Rivera and Freda Kahlo had hung out there. It was home to a community of American expatriates, artists and writers, and the site of a famous art school, the Instituto de Allende. The moment they arrived, they knew they didn't want to leave. It was such a magical and alluring place. The living was inexpensive and relaxing, a perfect place to retire. That was surely a fantasy that suited them both, but Peggy was pregnant and expecting in July. She didn't know she was going to have twins until it happened. In the meantime, the couple stayed as long as they could, enjoying the Shangri-la they had discovered.

By most standards, San Miguel was primitive, but it was romantic and charming, and life there made it easy to dream about what you genuinely wanted and what you could have. Ron and Peggy were both no-frills individuals who didn't mind roughing it. On the drive down, they had camped along the way, and once they had crossed into Mexico, they afforded themselves the luxury of a cheap hotel here and there. They were happy to make sacrifices in order to save money. Ron's pension wasn't much, but it provided them with the opportunity for time and freedom, as long as they stayed on a budget. There was a popular travel guide coming out at the time: *Fodor's Mexico on $5 a Day.* That was the blueprint. They knew that having children would make it a lot harder, but it was a challenge they both accepted and agreed upon. They were committed to making it work, whatever it took.

They were reluctant to leave Mexico, but all good honeymoons must end eventually. The twins popped out on American soil, and Julie was born the following summer. Four years later in 1968, it was quite a different picture. They were now a family of five, and Ron and Peggy decided it was time for a trip back to San Miguel. We made the journey in our first VW van. For Amy and me, the experience wasn't completely new; we'd had a taste of Mexico from the womb, and it always felt familiar and nourishing to be there. That original VW was a used clunker. It looked cute and fun, like a toy, with sixteen windows and a small pop-up roof and full-sized tent that attached to the side. It housed all of us comfortably. Slowly and clumsily, the funny old van chugged and rattled down the interstates and the bumpy roads, carrying us to Mexico and back, eventually, at its own lackadaisical pace. Overall, it was a successful trip regardless of the unexpected mishaps and detours. We had a wonderful summer, and in 1970 we returned again in our second used VW. We were growing bigger and heavier with more stuff to haul along, but we made the pilgrimage, staying on course and slowly but surely arriving at our distant destination happy and together.

We spent the whole summer in San Miguel, then turned around, and drove back to New Jersey in time to begin our first year of school. That second VW broke down more than once along the way too. It was all part of the adventure. We learned to take the good with the bad and have a memorable time regardless of the inevitable ups and downs of life on the road. It was obvious, however, that the family was going to need a newer, stronger vehicle if they insisted on keeping up the lifestyle. Ron and Peggy loved all the features of the VW camper; there was no question it was the vehicle that suited them best, but they still hadn't found one they could totally rely on. Finally, they dedicated themselves to save up for a brand-new model. It would take two more years.

Gradually and through much trial and error, the family was perfecting the art of camping and traveling comfortably. The three of us kids stretched out in back for the long drives. We pulled into KOA campsites for a short rest, unpacked the van, popped up the roof, stayed a few days, then moved on to the next state and the next one. There was plenty of room for everybody. It took a week or so to make the long drive to Mexico, but we had the whole summer to relax and make ourselves at home in San Miguel once we arrived. We found an ideal little house located on the grounds of the Instituto that we rented for practically nothing. Dad took his painting classes; he even got paid to teach one or two to earn a few extra pesos. The following year, our second van wasn't up for the long trip back to Mexico and we stayed in the States. We did manage a drive down to Florida at Christmas, but the car was running poorly. We sold it as soon as we made it back home, and in the meantime, we bought an old Volvo to get us through the rest of the winter. It was weird being without a van for a while—like a turtle without its shell. The Volkswagen camper had become our family identity, regardless of whichever one we owned or drove. You definitely grow attached to it; you feel homesick without it. You long for its comfort and familiarity, its maternal warmth and assurance. It wouldn't be long, however, before we had another one.

By the late spring of 1972, Ron and Peggy had enough money to buy their dream model. It was ordered from Germany and delivered to Baltimore in May. They purchased the brand-new VW bus for $3,600 cash. It was light blue. It wasn't a camper yet; it was just a basic bus with two bench seats in back. Ron immediately drove it out to a factory in Indiana, where it was converted into what they called a Sportsmobile. The conversion took a couple weeks. The center bench seat was removed and the back seat was turned into a folding sofabed. The pop-up roof was installed, which pushed straight up, creating a loft bed big enough for two. That's where Amy and I slept. Julie was still young and tiny enough to fit into a hammock that clasped across the driver and passenger seats, and Mom and Dad took the sofabed downstairs. It was similar to what we had been used to, but the engine was much stronger. It was a brand-new vehicle with a blank odometer and its whole life ahead of it. We couldn't wait to see what it could do! The side tent fit it perfectly, and we could sleep in there when it rained or

when we wanted more space to really stretch out and make ourselves at home. The tent was tall enough to stand up in. When
we'd stay anywhere for a few days or more, we unloaded all our
stuff into the big tent, laid out our sleeping bags, and used it as a
kind of family room. Otherwise, we all slept in the van for brief
stops when we had to get on the road early the next day.

Many times we drove at night. The sofabed was laid out and
us kids slept sideways across it like three pigs in a blanket. Mom
and Dad could put on more miles after we were asleep and all
calmed down. They shared a thermos of coffee and took turns
driving, even switching places in mid-flight on a couple occasions—without stopping to pull over. That was a fancy trick they
always bragged about. It was better to keep the gentle lull of the
engine purring and steady into the night, which prevented any of
us from waking up and having to go to the bathroom. It was a
neat experience to open our eyes to a fresh new part of America
every morning, still humming along, the first rays of light peeking
over the horizon. The scenery had completely changed overnight.
What a way to start the day! The weather got warmer the farther
south we went. We pulled into the next new campsite and Mom
and Dad set everything up as soon as we arrived. Us kids went
out and explored while they arranged our little homestead. We
had all day to run around and do as we pleased. We met other
kids, played outdoors, and were free to have as much fun as we
wanted. Our parents didn't care what we did. It was safe; it was
never boring. It was summer camp on wheels. We didn't know
how lucky we were, how much freedom we had. For us, it was a
normal life, to keep seeing new places and meeting new people,
and then moving onward to somewhere new.

Soon enough, we were on the road again and full steam ahead.
Once we got going, we rarely stopped for meals. Peggy climbed
in back when Ron was driving and prepared our mid-flight meal.
We had egg salad sandwiches and Hi-C and cookies, a picnic on
wheels. After lunch, Mom packed everything back up and we kept
speeding along. We progressed from state to state at a good steady
pace through Ohio, Kentucky, Tennessee, Alabama, Arkansas,
Mississippi, Louisiana, and Texas. When we finally crossed the
border into Mexico, it was suddenly a completely different world,

but we got used to the culture shock gradually, and we started to remember how Mexico was, and it felt exciting and familiar again the deeper we entered.

The brand-new van was already logging some big miles. It was a lot faster and peppier than the previous VWs, but the new car seemed to be experiencing some peculiar electrical problems. A fuse burned out—and then another one. After we picked up the Sportsmobile in Indiana, I told my parents that I was getting shocked sitting in the car. It happened when we pulled into a rest stop for a break. Mom told me it was static electricity. But then Dad thought he felt something too. They ignored it and got back on the road. Pretty soon everybody started experiencing strange fuzzy sensations. Something was definitely wrong. Every time we stopped, it happened again. It was an invisible mystery, but it was definitely real. Finally, we had to go to a garage and have the weird problem investigated. Amy and I started freaking out, and when they let us out of the car, we didn't want to get back in. We were stranded in the sticks of Kentucky for a few days, and eventually someone was able to figure out the cause of the problem. We were all a little jumpy after that and afraid to touch anything metal. Mom told us to keep our tennis shoes on. "Why do we have to keep our tennis shoes on?" She said, "Just in case." Somehow that advice was not reassuring, but eventually things got back to normal and we were on our way again.

That problem was soon forgotten when Ron started noticing that the new van was consuming an awful lot of motor oil. It was gulping it up like lemonade. Every time we pulled into a filling station, the attendant checked the oil, and it always needed another quart or two. That couldn't be normal, and it definitely wasn't. Ron stuck his head under the car and tried to find a leak. Where was it all going? He was getting annoyed, "This is a brand-new car, for Christ's sake!" Half-way to Mexico, a thousand miles from home, loaded up with all the kids and everything else, this wasn't supposed to be happening. The whole point of having bought the new car was to not have to worry about stupid crap like this anymore, he complained to Mom. Well, what do you expect from a VW? It became an emergency that could no longer be ignored. In Tupelo, we visited the birthplace of Elvis and we had lunch in a nearby park. Afterwards, Mom and Dad had a serious talk about what to do next. The car had problems that weren't going away. They could turn around and drive it all the way back to the dealer. They deserved that much. It was under warranty. For all their troubles, they could take this lemon—now converted into a Sports-lemon, back to Baltimore. Hell, all the way back to Germany! That was what they should have done. That is what most people would have done. That was the reasonable—albeit inconvenient thing to do. But that is NOT what they did. That would have changed the course of history forever. That would have permanently erased the entire beginning, middle, and end of this entire story. It was obviously Peg's decision. Ron had little say in the matter, and we all remember the look on her face. She was pissed, but she was determined. "Get in the car!" she snapped. We looked at Dad. We hesitated. We were scared. She said, "Get in the goddamn car right now!" and we loaded up again. Then we drove onward and outward and we kept going just like we always had, and never looked back.

And that, as they say…has made all the difference.

Chapter 3

Oil and Lemon

The month-old van's electrical problems might have had some-thing to do with the interior reconstruction that was done on the vehicle in Indiana, but those folks had never touched the engine. The oil leak was clearly a manufacturer's defect. Canceling an entire summer vacation on account of some technical difficulties was out of the question. The only thing they could do if they wanted to stay on the road and stay on schedule was to keep putting oil in the car—so that's what they did. Neither Ron nor Peggy knew a thing about motors, but they had plenty of experience driving VWs on long trips. They knew how quirky they were, but it seemed no matter what went wrong it was usually never anything major. They crossed their fingers, kept the dipstick wet, and kept their sights to the road ahead until they got where they had set out to go. They stopped at various mechanics along the way in hopes that there was someone who could fix the problem quickly. But at every garage the advice was the same: It's a new car, take it back to the dealer. So they kept denying and kept heading south, pushing and praying full-speed towards the Mexican border. In Texas, the last mechanic they saw warned them that if they planned to go into Mexico, the warranty would cease to be valid. They held their breath and crossed the Rubicon.

Other than the trail of tears they were depositing beneath them, most of the car was running strong and fine. If worse came to worse, it was still habitable. They had all the comforts of home with them and could survive anywhere. They kept the faith and they kept moving. Ron was in awe of his wife. He had never seen anybody with such determination and drive. He realized it was futile to get in her way and he followed her commands like a loy-al first mate. We all looked up to her. Whatever she told us, we accepted, even when we were worried and scared. She erased all our doubts and she never took no for an answer. We were going to make it to Mexico and we were going to land on the moon. We were like astronauts in our vulnerable little pajama spacesuits, and she was our mission control. She was Houston, and our life was in her hands. It was going to be a nail-biter right until splashdown.

There is a great lesson here. Mom insisted that the only way to know if something is trustworthy or not is to trust it. That's the only way you find out. Peggy had more faith in that car than probably anything or anybody in the world. She knew she had to trust the van. Most people would have taken it back to the factory and washed their hands of it. But she didn't do that. And because she didn't do that the first time, she didn't do it the second time, or the third time, or ever. She kept believing and kept trusting and kept pushing forward. Most people don't have that kind of faith in a car. They believe there is some cruel or ironic rule in life that when you really need something, it will inevitably let you down. They believe it is foolish to trust a machine, but to her this special kind of faith was natural; it was her personal source of strength, a test of her will and character. She'd been abandoned before, by life, in a way, and that had made her determined to never let it happen again.

The VW may not have been built perfectly, but it could be re-built. With a little patience and optimism and understanding, it could be made stronger and better. There existed an uncanny bond between her mind and the car. Their inner workings contained the same driving force. It was intense at times; it was even spooky. She treated the car as if she depended on it for her survival. She helped it too. It needed to be made aware of its own potential. It needed coaxing, patience, encouragement, tough love, a kick in the pants—the kind only a real mother can provide. She understood that it wasn't automatically born with that self-awareness, that sense of sureness and dependability. It took time and practice, trial and error, uphill battles, tests and tribulations. It might take years to become what it was truly capable of being. If the car broke, you repaired it. It broke again and you repaired it better—until it broke less and less, and finally could withstand anything, and never be defeated. For forty-four years she propped that vehicle up, supported it, pushed it, loved it. It owed her for that, and in return, the car responded in kind—if you think that's possible; if you believe that a car can trust you back, and remain faithful and true and loyal to its owner. It can!

The keep-replacing-the-oil strategy held out for the last and hardest part of the long journey. The car was maxed out as far as its capacity and load were concerned and Peggy kept stretching it to its limits. The final test was traversing the treacherous mountain passes of central Mexico. The road was deteriorating and narrow, with dozens of blind curves and no railings. One more rainstorm and there wouldn't even be a road; it was literally eroding off the cliff. I remembered that drive like a nightmare. I was absolutely petrified. I clung to the floor of the car and refused to look out the window. It was a thousand-foot drop-off to an empty canyon below. I thought we were going to die for sure. I was only eight years old; I was too young. The morbid headlines flashed across my mind: "Family of Five Plummet to Their Deaths: Oil Leak Suspected."

Peggy never blinked. She was a fearless and competent driver. She insisted on tackling the villainous mountain single-handedly, and Ron let her do what she did best. We made the final steep climb late at night. It was black as hell, no other cars, no lights, nobody except us, winding around the mountain in the dead of night, tightroping the abyss. When the worst part was finally over, we saw the dimly speckled lights of San Miguel in the distance. It was like seeing angels at the end of a tunnel. We were safe. We were there. We had arrived.

Chapter 4

Nuts and Bolts

We stayed at the small campsite outside of town for a week until we found a place to rent for the summer. It was an unfurnished little casita on Calle Indian Muerto with a place for the van behind the walls off the street. By the time we unloaded the car and moved everything inside, the house was practically furnished. That's how much stuff Mom had packed. She even brought her sewing machine and sewing table, and she got to work making curtains for the van. That was a personal gesture of gratitude. It was a sign we were going to keep her for a long time. We settled in our new home, with three months ahead to stay and peacefully enjoy the summer.

We already knew San Miguel well by now. It was our third summer there and even though it was getting more popular every year with Americans and other visitors, the town still felt like it was our own little secret. There were very few cars in those days. The new VW was great for climbing the steep and bumpy streets. San Miguel is small enough to walk everywhere, but Mom was always driving the van around like a nosy explorer finding the best deals and better opportunities. We took a lot of field trips. We visited Guanajuato to see the volcano ruins and the mummy museum, and we regularly went to the natural springs outside of town for a refreshing swim. The old Mexican lifestyle suited us very comfortably. The original arts and crafts produced by the local artisans adorned our little house. Everything was so colorful and bright: the fruits and vegetables and flowers and blankets, even the ancient town walls were painted pink and blue and bright yellow. The local inhabitants lived simply and traditionally, the same way they had for hundreds of years. They were poor by American standards, but by no means were they miserable. They seemed very content and subdued, and yet they were always open to a lively celebration and living life at a slow and easy pace. The months we spent there were pure and unspoiled, and from day to day nothing ever seemed to change. It was vibrant and magical and serene. You didn't want to be anywhere else. You didn't want to ever leave. You wanted to stay there forever and be happy.

At the end of June, the summer rains came. There was the deep gentle purr of thunder far in the distance, and it was warm enough to keep the shutters open all night and smell the sweet scent of the rain gently tapping upon the ceiling and the patio floor. In the mornings it was sunny and hot and fresh, and the showers had cleaned away the dust in the streets, and the plants and flowers were shiny and colorfully blooming. It was so tranquil and soothing. The modern world seemed as if it had yet to be invented, centuries away in a distant land, in the far, far future.

Ron was happy to paint every day. He was out at the Instituto or in the Jardin, making watercolors of the churches and gardens and colonial buildings, and portraits of the old blind beggar in the square or of the women selling fruit and flowers at the market. Amy and I took arts and crafts classes at the Instituto as well. We made friends and were learning Spanish and we roamed freely around on our own, exploring every part of the quaint and fascinating old town. It was a very safe and protective place, and a lovely place to experience life without stress or worry.

It was a very unique experience for us kids. Our parents weren't off to work every day. There was no television, and we were immersed in a very different culture that was always amazing and authentic and new. The soundtrack was all in Spanish, the food was exotic, and every day we were exposed to a variety of different sights and sounds and tastes and smells. Compared to the houses in the suburbs of New Jersey, our meager dwellings looked like ancient ruins. We didn't have all the fancy and modern stuff Americans had back home. We were out of the loop of the constant rat race and mundane responsibilities most people dealt with. If Mom and Dad had been much younger, we wouldn't have had that lifestyle. America was going through prosperous times with so much technology and growth and material gains. They were putting a man on the moon. But our existence seemed to be going backwards, into the past. It was better. Mom was always telling us to think originally, not to expect the same common and trendy things as everybody else, to be unique. It rubbed off on us in the long run, even though at the time we felt a bit awkward and insecure and a little weird compared to our peers. When we got back to the States, we appreciated the two different worlds. We learned to adapt to new changes and we were able to make friends easily under all kinds of circumstances. It was an education that had a unique and artful impact on our lives and how we turned out.

Bad things happened too. We got diarrhea, the electricity went out for almost a week. Julie broke her leg quite badly. It was the third time she had broken her leg and she was only seven years old. We were visiting the outdoor market one afternoon at the top of town, when a downpour suddenly hit. One minute it was hot and sunny, and before you knew it, there was thunder and lightning clapping down. We were trying to get Julie in the back seat of the car when her shoe came off. The inundation of rain had suddenly created a river of floodwater rushing down the narrow street. Her shoe got taken away by the rapid current and disappeared downstream faster than anybody could chase after it. We lost our grip on Julie, and she fell hard on the cobbled street. We immediately got her to the local doctor, who wrapped her in a plaster cast up to her waist. She had a fractured femur. That was a major setback which occurred early in July. At least we had the van, which fortunately offered enough space to be able to transport her around in a stretched-out position. For the rest of the summer, she slowly healed. It made life harder for everybody, but it could have been worse. At least we were all together as a family and we were in a beautiful place on vacation. Mom hired a local girl named Lola to be our babysitter. We picked up a cheap wheelchair for Julie that fit in the van. Lola took us to the park and she taught us Spanish nursery rhymes and games and we ate ice cream every day.

Eventually it was time to see about getting the van's engine looked at. There was a VW mechanic in the next town over. Ron went there alone and found the garage, and he was able to communicate (más o menos) what the problem was with the oil leak. He left the car with the mechanic, who told him to come back in a day or two. Ron hopped on an old, second-class bus going back into San Miguel that stopped at every little ranch along the way. He finally made it back to town but it seemed to take forever. It was the first time we had been without the family car. It had become an irreplaceable part of our life, and the thought of not having it was unimaginable. Hopefully, the mechanic could figure out how to fix it.

Now we've all heard of "Mexican time," and it is no exaggeration to say that you've got to have the patience of a monk when it comes to how long things can take. The last thing you want to be is a demanding foreigner. There is a good reason for that. The native peoples of Mexico experienced a cruel history of being abused and enslaved by their Spanish overlords. As a result, they often respond with indifference or what might appear as "laziness" when you start getting impatient and pushy. You can't blame them, and you have to keep that in mind and see things from their point of view. In America, in the modern world, we learn that time is money. In Mexico, it's a different story. Don't make demands; it only upsets the people, and it's not culturally appropriate.

Ron went back to the shop several days later. It wasn't a garage really, just a house with some old VW's parked on the street in front. The mechanic's wife answered the door and she called out to her husband who appeared and greeted Ron. He had a big, half-silver, half-toothless grin, and his face and hands were covered with black grease; he looked like a coal miner. He seemed very happy and pleased with himself. He managed to convey to Ron that he had located the cause of the problem. "Oh, good!" Ron said. The mechanic led him back to another room which was more or less the living room of his house. He said proudly, "There!"

Ron couldn't believe what he saw. Before him, all scattered about the living room floor on a plastic tarp, was every single nut and bolt of the entire engine, laid out piece by piece. The whole damn motor had been removed from the now-empty shell of the van, which was out on the street in front, soulless and inert. Ron's only reassurance was the fact that the guy had marked and labeled all the parts. Needless to say, the car wasn't ready yet. But the good news was that he had apparently found the cause of the problem, and he would be able to fix it and put it all back together. So, don't worry.

Ron didn't hear the man. His entire life was whizzing by, like a Volkswagen with an engine. He kept thinking…this is a brand-new car, it's only two months old. I'm in the middle of nowhere on a chicken bus, with a retarded daughter who is in a cast up to her sternum, and we won't be able to make it back to the States, even on a donkey. But he knew he had no choice other than to trust this fellow and hope he was competent. The gentle man's self-assurance and friendliness at least made Ron feel a little more at ease, but he was still sweating. He managed to produce a nervous smile. They sat down in the kitchen and the wife made them a bite to eat. Ron acted as pleasant and polite as he could be without knowing a word of Spanish. Even if he did, what could he say? His fate lay completely in the grease-worn palms of this other man. Finally, Ron gestured, "Mañana-mañana?" which was the only way he knew to communicate: "The day after tomorrow? Possible?"

The mechanic said, "Easy. No problem."

Ron responded with the stiff upper lip of an Englishman, "Jolly good, then." He tipped his head, said goodbye, and then caught the next rickety bus back to San Miguel by nightfall.

"Where's the car?" Peggy asked.

"It's not ready."

"Well, did he say when it was going to be ready?"

Ron said, "In a couple days. But he's found the problem."

"What was the problem?"

"It's complicated."

"You don't understand any Spanish!" Peggy said. "Do you want me to go back there with you?"

"No! I'll go back in a couple days."

He waited four days, just to be sure. When he got there, the whole engine was put back together and the car was ready and waiting for him. The amazing thing was the guy didn't even want to charge Ron for the work. He had taken so much satisfaction in having solved the conundrum, that was enough for him. It didn't need any parts, just to be reassembled the way it should have been in the first place. Ron insisted on giving him something, but it couldn't have been much. They shook hands and Ron drove the car back into town, and that was the end of the leaking oil. It was a great relief. Everything was okay. The van was back safe at home with the family, and they felt like a complete unit again.

In the decades that followed, Ron and Peggy returned to that same mechanic many times. They had a good friendship that lasted for years. Peggy didn't know much Spanish herself, just basic vocabulary, but between them they were able to figure things out, and to understand and like each other. That was the most important thing. It was the start of some good karma that continued for a lifetime.

Chapter 5
Ay, Chihuahua!

For three summers San Miguel de Allende was the family's second home. In the center of town is El Jardin (The Garden). Across from the park is a beautiful and famous Spanish-style cathedral known as the Paroquia. There are ornate iron benches and shady trees and a small gazebo in the center of the square. Before sunset in the *tarde,* the trees all fill with singing birds. It's a very peaceful time. The church is a popular site for festivals and weddings and holiday events, and every Sunday the local townsfolk gather there before and after Mass. Vendors sell colorful balloons and toys and candy and the families are always together. The square is blocked off to traffic and children are running about, playing and chasing each other. The weekend evenings can be quite festive. Mariachis play traditional Mexican songs, and people are singing along and clapping and dancing. There are fireworks in the square every summer and on Mexican Independence day in September. In the early years on Saturday nights, it was the local custom for the young people to meet in the Jardin. Dressed in their nicest clothes, the boys and girls slowly strolled around the square in opposite directions, eyeing each other bashfully in passing, occasionally stopping to say hello or chat, when they got up the nerve.

One evening, a van full of young American hippies showed up in the square. They were all barefoot and shirtless and had their radio turned up loud. That didn't go over well. The police station was on the corner, and a Mexican cop came out and immediately confronted the unwelcome visitors. He chastised them for their disrespectful appearance and behavior. "What do you think this place is?" he told them. "Put on your clothes! Don't ever show up here looking like that!" The hippies acted perplexed. "Que pasa? What's the big deal, man?" But the Mexican chief was very serious. The hippies got in their van and were forced to move on, and that was that.

Since long before Ron and Peggy ever bought a VW van, the iconic vehicle had already earned a somewhat dubious reputation. Mexicans are poor, but they're not usually nomadic and they don't live in their cars. During the Vietnam War, the American draft dodger presence in Mexico gave the VW a kind of bad rap. It was a stigma that was hard to shake, and Ron and Peggy were constantly at risk of being pulled over by the federales. It happened on more than one occasion. But once the local cops took a look at the older couple and their children, and realized they didn't fit the mold, everything was usually okay. For a lot of years, however, they had to be careful because the Mexicans didn't want that element in their country.

In all the times that Ron and Peggy took their van into Mexico, nothing bad ever happened to them. They loved the people and the country and the Mexican culture. Compared to life in the States, Mexico was a tranquil escape. It felt ancient and timeless. The family and the van spent a great majority of their years there, and the local people always took good care of them. Whenever they left Mexico, Ron always said to Peggy how sad it was to leave. The van is Mexican at heart. The country and the people are a big part of its history, its personality, and its character. Ever since the engine was put back together by that first mechanic who rescued it from an early demise, the VW owes a debt of gratitude and respect to the Mexican people. It was a good vibe, "Buena Onda," as they say.

At the end of the summer, it was finally time to drive back to the States. Julie had been in a cast for two months, and although still delicate and very skinny, she was on the mend. Before heading straight home, however, Mom and Dad decided to make a last-minute detour. After having spent three months in the mountains, it was time to see the coast. We packed up everything again and descended westward to the Pacific ocean. We passed through Guadalajara and stayed at Lake Chapala for a couple nights, and from there it was all downhill until we reached Puerto Vallarta a day or so later. It was sticky and hot in Puerto Vallarta, but there were coconut trees and gold sand beaches and tropical waters.

In addition to our family of five, the VW carried another passenger. In San Miguel we had adopted a stray dog, a puppy that was half-Chihuahua and half-Pekinese. Mom and Dad let us keep the new pet while we stayed in San Miguel but told us that we would have to leave her in Mexico once we started back for the States. That was the agreement. But after a couple months of growing attached, it was impossible to abandon her. We begged Mom to let us take the dog home with us. No, that was simply out of the question. They would confiscate the dog at the border. You can't bring a stray dog into the United States without any shots or papers. The best-case scenario would be that the dog remain in quarantine for six months—so forget it. But we begged and complained, and Mom finally agreed that we could take her with us to the beach, but no farther than that.

It was Dad's idea to name the dog Perri, short for *perrito,* which means "little dog." Perri was a weird but happy dog that had some peculiar idiosyncrasies. She chased her tail obsessively, convinced that she was being pursued by an invisible predator. She constantly ran around in circles to guard herself from the attacks. Frequently, she caught the rascal, and bit her own tail, which was always bleeding and torn up. Perri had the bug-eyes of a typical Chihuahua, but the long hair of a Pekinese. Her soft fur had a nice golden-brown color. Peri's most redeeming quality was that she smiled. When Perri was excited to see you, she produced a wide and genuine grin that showed all her teeth. She had nice teeth, not mean or hostile fangs, but a really contagious and friendly smile. It was so cute. You never saw a dog smile like that, and how could you turn down the adorable creature when she radiated such appreciation and glee? That's how she got food, and love, and that's why we had taken her in from the street. We gave her warm milk and she smiled at us. After that, she became part of the family.

On the morning we arrived in Puerto Vallarta, an interesting event occurred. We had been driving through the night, and at sunrise we finally arrived at the beach. The family all unloaded from the car, and we took Perri for a walk along the sand. Afterwards, Mom decided the family deserved a nice breakfast out. We went to a cafe, but we couldn't take the dog. So, we strapped

Perri's leash to the steering wheel and left her in the front seat with the windows slightly cracked. When we came back half an hour later, Perri was gone. Obviously, she couldn't have untied herself; she must have been kidnapped! We tore the car apart looking for Perri, but she was gone. Amy and I cried and cried. Julie was speechless. Mom and Dad scratched their heads.

Ron was practical. "We can't take the dog back with us, anyway. Oh well, kids. Better now than later." Mom should have felt the same way, but Peggy didn't like being taken advantage of and she immediately suspected foul play. She started down the street and went to every house and every store. She was relentless, knocking on door after door. Dad and us kids waited in the van, hoping Mom would find Perri. But Dad was getting impatient. He said it was pointless, and time to move on. Finally, Mom returned to the car. She had a fierce look in her eye. She said the lady in that store was lying, she could feel it. She didn't trust her. Mom said that she was going to go back in there and take another look. She came back out to the car a minute later and said, "They've got Perri in there! I can hear her whimpering. I'm gonna go back and get her. Ron, come with me."

But Ron didn't want any trouble. Besides, he had to stay with the kids, so nobody would steal us too. Peggy said, "Fine. I'm going in!" A minute later, she came out running with Perri clasped in her arms, the leash dragging from the dog's fragile little neck. "Start the car, Ron! Hurry up! Start the car!" The whole family quickly jumped in the van and burned rubber out of there before the police showed up or somebody came out wielding a butcher's knife. It's not a crime to steal back a dog who was kidnapped in the first place, but you've got to respect the culture. Perri was Mexican after all. Was it fair for us to take her as our own? As the van raced away, Mom recounted what had happened inside. She said she had spotted Perri in the backyard strapped to a tree. She then leapt behind the counter and quickly untied the vulnerable mutt. The owner suddenly appeared, but she couldn't say anything. "She knew she was guilty. So I took her back." Mom was a hero! We were all cheering. Ron had been through a war, and even he was amused by his wife's bravery. Peggy was always a fighter. She never gave up her ground.

We stayed at the beach for a few relaxing days, and then it was definitely time to begin the long drive back. It had been a memorable vacation. We had seen and done an awful lot in three months. The van felt like a central member of our family now, and so was our new loveable little pet dog. From the southwest coast of Mexico to the northeast coast of the United States is a long drive, but the oil leak problem was all solved and the van was running strong. We sped north to the U.S. border, happy to be on our way home. But how could we abandon Perri now, after saving her life? Dogs are like cars: you just don't give up on them when the going gets tough, and Mom didn't make us leave Perri behind. We got closer to the border. We were scared and excited at the same time. Smuggling was a dangerous business. Mom and Dad told us they could be arrested and held in a Mexican jail. "We understand," us kids nodded, "We'll take the chance." We begged and pleaded, "Please, Mom! Please!" Our parents looked terribly concerned. They were annoyed too, and yet there was mercy in their eyes. Finally they threw up their hands. "Okay," they said. "We'll see what happens..."

Now when you re-enter the United States with a van loaded from floor to ceiling, it is at the full discretion of the Mexican authorities to totally search the vehicle. If they want, they can (make you) take the whole car apart and there's nothing you can do about it. The only thing Ron and Peggy had going for them was that they didn't look like drug traffickers and there were no peace signs dangling from the rearview mirror. A few miles from the border, we pulled over and rehearsed the game plan. When we got to the customs crossing, Dad would produce the car's papers, answer any questions calmly, cooperate and act nonchalant. Us kids were not to utter a peep. Perri was hidden under some blankets behind the back seat. Nobody would move. If the car ended up being searched and the dog discovered, everybody would just act surprised and say, "What's that? A dog? A Mexican dog? How did that get there? It must have snuck in and stowed itself away without our knowing. How sneaky! We swear, officer, we have never seen that mutt before."

All was going smoothly. The customs official checked the vehicle registration, the insurance, and the visa papers. Everything seemed to be in order. He looked the van up and down and poked his head in back, assessing our innocent childhood faces. He was thinking about his upcoming coffee break. He stroked his mustache a few times and tugged on his gun belt. Then he said what they always say: "Are you bringing any fruits or vegetables?"

"No, sir." It looked like we were going to be given the green light. Then for some inexplicable reason, probably because I thought I was being helpful, I opened my big mouth and blurted out, "What about those bananas?"

My parents both turned white.

"Bananas?" the official asked. "You have bananas?"

"No. We don't have any bananas. We already ate them."

The guard hesitated for another moment. He certainly was macho. We all held our breath. Finally, he said, "Bueno," and waved us through into the United States.

I had come within an inch of my life that day, and barely escaped a severe lashing with a coarse leather dog leash. But we were home free! Perri had successfully immigrated to the U.S.A. She didn't have her papers—but what else is new? She was with us. We sped up the interstate, on our way back home—one big, happy, and intact family. It had been the first big adventure in the new van, and a trip to remember.

Chapter 6

All Packed Up

It was a regular spring tradition to systematically pack the van and prepare for the next big summer trip. The process had to be organized and efficient, and Mom was just the person for the job. Nobody else was going to do it. She started planning two months in advance. First, she packed everything the family definitely needed. After that, it was everything we might need. Finally, she crammed in all the stuff that would be nice to have and that we wished we had brought. Her strategy was to fill the car with as much as she could. Most of it was all tucked away and out of sight. Dad always complained that we were taking too much damn junk. He didn't think the engine could handle it. There was probably a maximum capacity when it came to the weight load, which Peggy obviously ignored. The interior itself was very big and roomy. There was a lot that could be stashed under the back seat and behind the driver and passenger seats. There was a good-sized shelf at the ceiling in back that held most of our clothes. That meant all the clothes and shoes five people needed for any weather conditions. Under the sink were drawers for the kitchen supplies, and there were two giant bins containing all our food, which could be used as seats with cushions on them. We had a luggage rack on top too, that carried a durable canvas bag strapped down with bungee cords. The view to the rear window had to be totally unobstructed; it was bad enough having to deal with three hyper kids behind the driver. We weren't ever strapped into any seatbelts, and we got up and moved all around and switched positions and bounced up and down like monkeys. It drove my parents crazy. The side mirrors were indispensable. They were constantly being monitored and adjusted. For some reason, they never seemed to stay in place. That was the co-pilot's duty, as well as reading the map and providing coffee and directions to the driver.

When we finally hit the road, Mom had packed all our clothes, blankets, pillows, everything required to prepare, store, cook and eat food, utensils and plates and pots and pans, glasses, cups and mugs, aluminum foil and plastic bags. We needed matches, lanterns, flashlights, an alarm clock, thermometer, cough syrup, aspirin, toothpaste, paper towels, and bathroom tissue. The van was equipped with a sink and a five-gallon supply of fresh water. There was the foldable cooking stove, a plug-in kettle, a thermos, fishing poles, tackle, tools for the engine, an ax, umbrellas, rope and clothesline, soap, batteries, maps, travel guides, playing cards, dominoes, hula hoops, Barbie dolls, and birthday candles, sewing supplies, art supplies, sunscreen, band-aids, sponges, rags, brooms and brushes, iron wool, dishwashing liquid, tacks and nails and screws and stakes, plastic tablecloths with clips to hold them to the picnic tables, a tent, a tarp, sleeping bags, flares, a spare tire, jack, and fuses. There were tiny bottles of creme-de-menthe, sherry, and Kahlua, as well as windbreakers, wool socks, gloves, sunglasses, reading glasses, wine glasses, camera, film, transistor radio, flip-flops for the whole family, Vicks vapo-rub, dentine, putty, string, rubber bands, paperback novels, Pepto-Bismol, a bucket, a squeegee, an iron, ironing board, scrabble board, folding beach chairs, a fondue set, Christmas lights, wrapping paper, a frisbee, small dog with leash, and a family of five. We were bound to forget something...

There is nothing like having the comforts of home when you're on the road. It makes all the difference. We had our little toys and games, like Monopoly and Parcheesi, that kept us occupied and entertained while Mom and Dad piloted the vehicle. We had plenty of room to stretch out our legs or lie down if we wanted; we could take a nap or sit up and watch the endless scenery going by. At night, we had curtains for privacy. There was even a curtain that separated the driver from the van's back cabin. When it got dark and quiet, we listened to our parents whispering and sipping their hot coffee as they drove through the night. To the rumbling and steady rhythm of the road, we dozed off into dreamland.

After driving all morning, it became the custom to pull over at a rest stop, stretch out our legs, have a bite, and see who else was on the road. It was a kind of social hour for us. In those days, there were plenty of families traveling up and down and across the continent, camping and exploring and going everywhere, just like we were. There were always other kids to meet and play with wherever we stopped. A lot of these families drove station wagons and pulled trailers. For the most part, American families preferred American cars, even though there were lots of VWs on the road too. Mom was an innovator when it came to furnishing the inside of the van for long-distance family travel. Most people never imagined how much the VW could hold and how roomy it was compared to other large cars. As kids, it was our little fort on wheels. We saw a car that had broken down, and there was a big family of kids running around in a field next to the highway, the dad stuck under the car trying to fix it. Other travelers were stopping to lend a hand, so we kept going. Those were the days when it seemed like all Americans wanted to go out and explore this great land of ours.

One time, we pulled over to help a young couple with an old Volkswagen that was stuck on the side of the road. The woman had a baby on her back. They had run out of gas on their way to a festival or concert. We made room for them inside and took them to the next gas station. We lent them our gas can, and then drove them back to their car. In that little emergency, we managed to squeeze eight people into the van. They were amazed at how prepared and comfortable we were. They were checking out Julie curiously and asked about her. We told them that we really didn't know what was wrong with her, that she couldn't say anything. They seemed fascinated. "I get it, man. She's just tripping on another plane," the guy said. "Maybe she'll come back one day." Then his woman said, "Or maybe she won't...maybe she likes it there, and that's cool." They both nodded approvingly.

Mom and Dad were too old to use words like "groovy" and "cool," but they were cool enough in their own way. They were just on a different path, man. They didn't listen to rock music or smoke grass, but they had a free spirit and good hearts. The young couple was able to get their van started and they thanked us for all our help. At that moment, Julie seemed to come out of her trance. She started giggling, and she waved goodbye to them, and everybody laughed. Later, Amy said to our parents,

"What were those guys talking about? Julie's not on a plane. She's in a car."

It's a different kind of plane," Mom tried to explain.

Dad said, "But they were correct. She's flying, all right."

We all looked at Julie. She was in her own deep thoughts again. She seemed to be reassessing what had just happened.

"I wonder where she is..." Amy said.

"She's with us!" Mom said quickly.

She was right. Julie may have been somewhere else mentally, in a time and a place we had no idea of. But she was also right here with her family, driving around the country in a Volkswagen van and seeing the world like everybody else.

Chapter 7

Driving to England

In the fall of '72 we were back in Mendham, New Jersey, for the start of school. The family took a drive up to the Maine coast in the early autumn to see the leaves changing color and to add a few more states to the roster. By December, we were on our way south to Florida for another Christmas vacation. The car's heater suddenly stopped working—a sign to head for warmer weather. We had taken our first VW down in '68 and camped at Jupiter beach, returned in '71 with the second one, and were back again with number three. This time, we drove all the way down to Key West. We stayed at a campsite right on the beach and settled in comfortably. We had plenty of room and plenty of time to relax and soak up the sun and enjoy the warm ocean. We even had a little Christmas tree with lights and tinsel that Mom had managed to stow aboard without anyone noticing. On Christmas morning, we awoke surprised and delighted to find a treasure of presents, all wrapped up and spread out under the little tree. There was no fireplace for Santa to come down, but he managed to find us. It was really neat celebrating Christmas in the sunshine and the outdoors, running around and playing on the beach and swimming in the ocean. We got to bring Perri with us, and she got a new leash with rhinestones and some nibbles in her stocking. It was a great Christmas and we had a wonderful time as a family. After the new year, we turned around and drove back north to the snow and ice. Grandma moved in with us for a while, but it was obvious Mom was itching to get out of New Jersey.

It was later that spring in 1973 that our parents announced we were moving to England. The trip was meant to be a year-long sabbatical. We sublet our house on Tempe Wick Farm to a family who agreed to take care of Perri while we were away. Ron had a sister in England with children and grandkids. There were other cousins and relatives there we had never met. Even though we had to leave Perri behind, there was never any question that the van was coming with us. After all, who goes to England and doesn't take their car? We reserved our accommodations on the Queen Elizabeth II, the luxurious ocean liner which had recently replaced the Queen Mary, now retired to Long Beach, California. The ship ferried our van and us across the Atlantic Ocean. It was quite an adventure and a memorable experience for everyone. We set sail on a warm evening in early June. Some friends of ours in New York were allowed to come aboard for the big bon voyage party before the boat left harbor. There was a rowdy and colorful celebration with champagne and streamers and everybody was drinking and living it up. The passengers were all waving at the crowd from the decks and there was a party in every cabin. Music was playing and people were dressed up in tuxedos and flamboyant costumes. Finally, when it was time to set sail, the friends had to depart the vessel, and the ship slowly pulled out of port and set sail into the evening. It was very exciting.

Ron was acting proud, having been a naval officer during the war. He and Mom were invited to meet the captain and the other officers onboard. Us kids were allowed to roam around and explore every fascinating corner of the ship. There were restaurants, bars, shops, hair salons, spas, a movie theater, and parties and events every day and every night. We ate gourmet meals and could enjoy as much food and drink as we wanted whenever we pleased. The ship was like a giant resort hotel with every kind of activity you could imagine. Five days later, we arrived in Southampton.

It was a very surreal experience to arrive in England and just drive our car off the huge ship and onto a foreign new continent. We were packed into the van as usual with all our belongings, totally equipped for a brand-new foreign adventure. Dad took the steering wheel and we disembarked onto land-ho. Waiting for us in his funny little English car was uncle Will, the husband of Ron's sister Olga. We followed him to their house, which was on Hayling Island near Portsmouth, a short drive from Southampton. It was a beautiful summer day. The sky was bright blue and the sun was shining. There were fields ripe with fresh strawberries along the road. Ron smiled and breathed in the fresh familiar air. We were all so happy. We couldn't believe we were in England! But Dad made one almost fatal error: he drove on the wrong side of the road. Of course, he knew better, he was from England. But the van had its steering wheel on the left side and he was distracted by all the excitement. We were cruising along happily on a scenic country road, admiring the strawberry fields and the panorama and everybody was honking at us. We thought they were honking to welcome us to England, like all the cheering we had enjoyed at the bon voyage. We barely avoided a head-on collision. Ron quickly snapped back to reality. It nearly became the shortest English vacation ever. Thankfully, the van and all of us within survived untouched, but it sure took our breath away!

Within a short time, we were at Aunty Olga's house, where we met all our cousins and second cousins, and we had a big family reunion. For the first week, us kids slept in the van in the driveway and Mom and Dad had a room inside the house. Soon enough, it was time to start exploring the English countryside and looking for a new home. The van was filled with everything we needed to camp for as long as it took to find a permanent place to settle down. We spent that whole first summer in the south of England, mainly in Cornwall and Devon. Mom and Dad wanted to find a home near the seaside. We drove all around and visited countless towns and villages. But England was a much more expensive place to live compared to where we had come from. In the beginning, there was no rush and we did a lot of sightseeing and exploring. But after several weeks of living out of the van, it became tiresome and not so fun. We had seen a lot and now it was time to get serious about finding a house. Mom and Dad were getting anxious. It was pretty obvious that Mom hated the food, and so did we. There were no McDonald's or Dairy Queens. We were cooking most of our meals on a camping stove in a field surrounded by sheep. Mom and Dad had to get food from inside the pubs, like steak and kidney pie and mashed potatoes, to bring out to us in the van. It got drizzly and cold day after day. In St. Ives, we almost moved into a flat over a fish and chips shop. Mom and Dad would have to run the shop. That didn't work out, and we kept looking. Finally, we gave up our dream of finding a nice little house on the seaside, and we headed into the city of London.

By now, the fall was upon us, and we would have to start school somewhere. London wasn't any cheaper than the countryside, and there were no campsites. Our first day in London, we drove around all day searching for an affordable hotel. It started getting dark and we had no idea where we were going to spend the night. We drove into a large park near the center of town in Chelsea. There we sat in the van, Mom and Dad figuring out what to do. A sign said the park closed at sunset.

There were no people anymore and suddenly night fell and it got very dark and quiet. We were right in the center of the busy city, in the eerie eye of an urban tempest. Everybody in London had somewhere to go home to—except us. There was nothing we could do except remain parked there until security came along and told us to move on. But nobody did, so we just stayed in the car in the dark, listening to the owls, and waiting. It didn't look like we were going to get any supper. Mom was too exhausted. She told us to stay very quiet and to try and close our eyes and go to sleep. We huddled together motionless under our blankets in the dark in the back of the van. Mom and Dad were trying to buy some time, but they were at the end of their rope. They sat in the front seats, not saying a word. We finally fell asleep, and they probably dozed off too eventually. It seemed as though we might actually be able to stay there until the early morning. Suddenly all hell broke loose!

There was a giant bomb blast from a theater directly across from the park entrance. The Irish Republican Army had set it off and a giant fire had erupted just a hundred yards away. There was pandemonium everywhere. Police and fire engines suddenly appeared and the whole scene was like a war zone. Ron started up the car to get the hell out of there. Us kids woke up screaming and crying. We could see the fire and all the commotion from the car, and hear the sirens, but the park entrance was blocked by all the emergency vehicles and there was no way to get out. In fact, due to all the chaos, nobody even noticed that we were there. We sat in the van, our mouths wide open, witnessing it all. Ron turned on the car radio and we quickly learned the news of what had happened.

The I.R.A. was claiming responsibility for the bombing. There had been numerous other such events in London in past weeks. With the break of dawn, the hysteria eventually started to settle down and we were able to drive slowly out of the park without being noticed. That is the only time I remember that we ever went "stealth"; by that I mean, not camping in a proper campsite, but just spending the night in the van. I doubt Mom or Dad got any sleep at all, but they saved the cost of an expensive hotel. It was a fantastic show and a very memorable first night in London. All that had been missing was the popcorn.

The next day we found lodging at a modest Bed and Breakfast that offered a decent weekly rate. It was the first and only hotel we had stayed in all summer. There we remained, while Mom and Dad made a daily search of London for a more permanent spot. The B & B was called Darlington House. It was right near Paddington Station and Hyde Park. We had one large room for the whole family. The lavatory was at the end of the hall, which you had to share with other guests. The hot and cold water to fill the bath came out of different faucets. Breakfast was served downstairs in the basement. They had hot bangers and mash every morning. On the top floor there was a TV room with dusty recliners where fuddy old Englishmen watched the news on the BBC. It was basically a boarding house with mostly permanent senior residents. It had its charm and a good central location in a very traditional part of town. There was a parking space for the VW off the street, where we could keep an eye on the van and have access to all our belongings. We basically lived out of our car, which was becoming pretty obvious.

We ended up staying at Darlington House for several weeks. It was cramped, but better than camping among the cow dung of Cornwall. The summer was over and it got cold and rainy every day. Mom had us enrolled at a public school in Westminster. Dad showed us the route by foot, and Amy and I walked to school every morning on our own. We walked right past Westminster Abbey along the way. We had abruptly been thrown into the fourth grade in a country that was quite different from what we were used to. But we adapted soon enough, and we started meeting other kids and fitting in. It wasn't long before we started to talk with a Cockney accent too.

But finding a school for Julie was going to be a lot tougher. Mom and Dad were having to take care of her while at the same time driving around London trying to find a place to live. It would have been a lot easier without Julie. Amy and me were always being threatened that we'd be sent to boarding school if we didn't behave. That's how they did things in England, apparently. It was like a Charles Dickens novel. One night, Amy confided to me that she had overheard our parents talking about putting Julie in a home. They had been discussing it seriously. Dad probably felt that under the circumstances, she was too much trouble. He was too old, and it was too difficult on the family. But Mom was adamantly against that. She was frustrated; she didn't want to accept that maybe it had been a mistake to come to England. Their notion of England was that it was going to be a romantic adventure with knights and castles and all that, but that's not how it was working out. Mom could be overly ambitious and stubborn. What was she after? Just a year earlier, the family had been in Mexico. What a dramatic contrast. Now the only thing that was remotely the same was the van. Thank God, at least, for the van. We could always drive away and escape, onto better and greener pastures. We'd never be stuck for long as dreary as things got.

We were constantly getting exposed to new experiences and seeing places and getting an education that most kids would never have. Every weekend we hopped in the van and traveled to other towns outside London, looking for a place to make our permanent home. Peggy was very picky and determined; she didn't want to end up in some lousy, uninspiring location. Even though we had little money, she believed that if you're persistent enough, the right opportunity will present itself and you should never settle for anything less. If you do, then you will resent it and be miserable, and you'll be stuck. So she kept looking and looking.

In late October, they finally found a place she liked. It was a half-hour outside of London on the Thames, between the counties of Middlesex and Surrey. It was a small house situated directly upon the banks of the river. It was a damp old place but the location was traditionally English and picturesque. Many of the neighboring homes were old houseboats that had been dragged up onto the banks to become permanent dwellings. The houses had names, like boats. Ours was called *Pentona,* which was its address. There were no street numbers because there wasn't a street; there was just our front yard and then the river. The Thames was our street. There were swans on the water and willow trees and boats slowly passing by. It was very romantic and Peggy said, "This is it!" and Ron agreed.

Pentona remained our home until 1975. We got pulled out of school in London and re-enrolled at a Church of England school across the river. We were half an hour outside of London. It was a nice pastoral stroll to school for Amy and me walking along the Thames. We used a key to get across the weirs and locks to the other side. The walk took a half an hour. Mom found a school for Julie too, and everything worked out as well as we could have hoped for. Without the VW camper we never would have had the money to make the big transition to a new life in England. The always dependable van got a well-deserved rest now. It had a nice private and safe space to park in the garden behind Pentona. We continued to make short field trips around England on holidays and weekends. It was nice to finally settle inside a real house for the cold and rainy winter. Soon it would be spring again, and Mom was already planning the next big summer adventure.

Chapter 8
European History

In 1974, the Chunnel had not been built yet. In order to get our van from England to France, we ferried it on a hovercraft, a very loud and obnoxious vehicle, best described as the bagpipes of transportation. We arrived on the shores of Normandy with everything we needed for a couple months of camping in Europe. Before departing, we saw the famous White Cliffs of Dover, and from there it was a quick and bumpy skip across the English Channel to Calais in the north of France. The first place I remember visiting was the trenches of World War I. Why anybody would want to be reminded of the horrors of that time and place in history seemed like a punishment, but if we hadn't seen it for ourselves, we probably never would have known about it or cared. Ron and Peggy's generations never forgot the World Wars. It was an obligation they strongly felt to honor those years soberly, to show and instill upon their children how destructive and wasteful and life-changing the first half of the century had been. We got right down in the muddy trenches where so many young soldiers had needlessly suffered and lost their lives. The day of the tour, the weather was drizzling and cold. The guide recounted all the horror stories in great detail: the stench, the rats, the gangrene, the shell shock, both sides shooting and blasting away at each other endlessly, in the dark, in the rain, only yards apart, for weeks and months on end until they were all slaughtered or maimed, broken and traumatized, defeated, dehumanized. It was ghastly, and that was the point. Mom was always reminding us how lucky we were. My dad never brought up the war. I asked him once how he had become a captain and a commander in the navy. I thought that was glamorous and heroic. He said people got killed and they needed to be replaced; it was that simple.

Once that was out of the way, it was on to more pleasant scenes of the countryside. It was important to Peggy that her children get a worldly education and have a variety of historical and cultural perspectives. One of the highlights of this trip for her was when we camped in France next to the Rhine River. She was very proud to get a camping spot right on its banks at a campsite near Strasbourg. She kept impressing on us kids that this was the famous Rhine River. "Remember this moment," she told us. Peggy had even packed her fondue set for the occasion. She had bought it years before when she had visited France and Europe as a young woman. Us kids thought the fondue tasted too much like wine, and Mom said that was the whole idea; it was supposed to warm you up. She explained that fondue was something you ate in the winter, not the summer, but we did it once just for the experience. We spent the majority of the summer camping in the south of France, visiting small villages and historic places and enjoying the warm weather. We went on to Spain next, then to Nice and the French Riviera, where Mom made sure we swam in the Mediterranean. Then we drove on to Switzerland to see the Alps before heading back.

The toughest drive the VW ever made was traversing the Pyrenees mountains. It was hell. The road was steep and unforgiving. There were noisy trucks that were spitting out gravel, and the constant dust made it practically impossible to navigate the road safely. The truck drivers were merciless and it seemed as if it was their intention to run everybody else off the road. It was a miracle that the van made it across and into Spain. The front windshield was scarred with pockmarks. Compared to the mountain passes of Guanajuato, it was much worse. We would have to find a way to avoid that route again when it was time to return.

In Spain, the family took a break from the hard driving, and the van was given a chance to lick its wounds. We camped on a beach on the north coast for two weeks at a place called Comillas, which literally means "quotation marks." It is in the Bay of Biscay between two prominent points that jut out. We took day trips to Santander and to Bilbao and explored the Spanish countryside in the north. We visited the caves at Altamira and saw the primitive paintings of bison and other wild animals made by cavemen that dated back 15,000 years. The caves had been buried and not discovered until the 19th century. Later, the site was closed to the public due to deterioration from all the tourist activity. That was another experience Mom had made sure we captured while we had the chance. There were countless time we wanted to call it a day after driving everywhere, but Mom would insist we go to one more place. We'd take a detour on some bumpy old road that was far out of our way. Looking back now, it was worth it to see all the things we might have missed, to fill each day to the brim. She took us wherever she knew was significant and historical and impressive. Dad was very well-read and well-traveled too. He knew the facts of all the places we visited and the biographies of the historic figures. We went to the town of Rouen, France where Joan of Arc had been burned at the stake. Mom believed in the importance of school, but she knew that more could be learned from traveling and seeing the world for yourself. To be in the actual place made the history more impactful and meaningful. It wasn't only about knowing and understanding the past, but about making your own history and having a well-rounded life and etching out a collection of memorable experiences for yourself. In the end, what else have you got?

Parents understand the benefit of reading their kids stories at bedtime, but for Mom, the picture book was the real world. Before we got tucked in every night, we had seen and lived a new adventure, a new chapter. She didn't lecture us about history, but she showed us what there was to see. In England, we had gone to Land's End and Stonehenge and the Tower of London. When we drove through Texas back in the States, we saw the Alamo where Davy Crocket was killed. We visited the landing spot of the May-flower and where the pilgrims had settled, and all the battle sites of the American Revolution. In Greenwich, England, we stood on the line that separates East from West, and we had our picture taken there with one foot in either hemisphere. I don't know how many times I learned a fact in school that I could relate to a trip we had made. I'd think, or I'd tell my teacher: "I've been there."

When Princess Margaret got married in London, we went in person to stand in the crowd next to Buckingham Palace and watch the royal carriages go by, waving our little Union Jack flags and cheering. I can still picture the procession; the carriages looked like they were built of solid gold. A few days later at school, the teacher asked the students what we had done over the weekend, and everybody said they had watched the wedding on the tele. I told her we had gone there in person, and my classmates seemed amazed, even though it was only twenty miles away from where we lived. It was those little efforts that Peggy took which made a big difference. I learned a lot about geography by tracing on the map all the small and significant places we had gone, connecting the dots into a larger picture. It was amazing that we were able to see so much in the Volkswagen, to actually drive right up to these places, slide open the door, and step out into a new world. We may not have appreciated it at the time, but these memories were more than snapshots. They were tactile experiences that would last a lifetime, with all the smells and tastes and feelings that went along with them. Peggy always wanted her feet and wheels on the ground and to be part of the landscape herself. She wanted miles on the odometer and worn-out tennis shoes. The VW was the vehicle that made it all possible, and more real. The car was a personal and essential part of our family. The experiences on the road got seared into our psyches and baked into our bodies, into our skin, our taste buds, our heads, our guts, the expressions on our faces, and the way we thought about everything.

These physical memories got built into the car itself too. Every mile driven and every terrain covered left its own legacy on the family van. Our van was an integral part of our identity; it was a member of the family. It had been to all these places with us and knew all the stories. It had seen all the sights and would continue to accompany us and get us wherever we went, and it looked forward as well to all that would come. It protected the family and carried us like a body carries its vital organs. It lived and breathed, it grew, it experienced, it thrived, it conquered, always moving forward. The van is a life; it's a biography that is as human and real as that of any person. It was one of us, and we were a part of it, too.

From Spain, we dipped down into the Mediterranean before circling back for a brief visit to Switzerland. The beaches of the Riviera were crowded and expensive. At Canne, we pulled into a campsite to take a quick look. A crazy and chubby little Frenchman in a bikini started tooting his whistle loudly at us. He looked like Picasso. He chased us on his little bicycle and kept shrieking his whistle. Apparently, the campsite was full and we weren't allowed to enter. My parents just wanted to do a lap and check the place out, but he was very angry and made us turn around and leave. From there, we skirted Italy, but didn't have time to visit. Mom and Dad just pointed from the van and said, "That's Italy over there. At least you can say you saw it."

There was one more important stop to make on our way back through France before summer's end. That was the town of Lourdes, famous for its holy waters. My parents decided that it was worth a shot to go there and see if we could get Julie cured of her autism. Julie had gone everywhere with us. She took in all the sights and sounds out the window and enjoyed the trips in the car wherever we went. She was a highly introspective individual. She was always in her own mind, thinking about who knows what, contemplating some great question. She would frequently rock her head and body back and forth to the rhythm of some interior beat that nobody else could sense. You could see in her eyes that whatever it was that engrossed her mind definitely amused her and kept her occupied and amused, but she was reluctant to ever share those thoughts. She never looked you in the eye directly, but she acknowledged us and she knew she was one of us. You were always in her periphery, it seemed, and not a priority to her. We were used to that by now, and none of us took it personally. Still, she did manage to display affection and warmth when it counted. Sometimes she started laughing and we never knew why. She was having a good time, at least, which was all that mattered. It may have been the case that Julie was supremely intelligent. She was obsessed with textbooks for some mysterious reason. Any textbook you gave her, she tore to pieces by consuming it with extreme freneticism, ripping the pages to shreds in the process of "reading." She wasn't angry at the book itself, but she was overly zealous, impatient, and ultimately negligent of its fragility—to the point where after finishing a book, she cast it aside indifferently, like a strangled dead chicken. Her pursuit of knowledge was insatiable, but she never was able to apply it. It was all just theoretical in her mind.

Julie had her regular spot in the back of the car where she sat in deep thought for hours at a time. Occasionally, she took a rest from reading, looked up for a few moments, and out the window at the passing landscape, contemplating it all, and making curious and knowing noises. She seemed to take pleasure in reflecting on the events of life, smiling occasionally, and experiencing genuine self-contentment. But most of the time, she kept reading and kept thinking, driven to find the ultimate meaning of it all. On Julie's ninth birthday, we arrived at Lourdes, where St. Bernadette had witnessed a miraculous vision of the Virgin Mary. Thousands of people who were handicapped or suffering had made the pilgrimage to Lourdes to bathe in the divine springs in an attempt to be cured, and many had experienced spontaneous healing on countless documented occasions. Just like them, we were going to dunk Julie in the holy water and see what happened. Julie could swim and always enjoyed going in the water with the rest of the family. We camped near the French village for a couple days and waited in line with the masses for the big chance at a miracle. Julie, herself, appeared highly skeptical. She probably thought it was us who needed to be fixed. We splashed water over her head and made a perfunctory attempt at praying as hard as we could. Unfortunately, it simply wasn't meant to be. Julie remained unperturbed and as self-satisfied as ever. We tried it a couple times, but there was pressure to keep the line moving. We dried her off, and said, "Oh, well." Everything was still okay. She was who she was, and that was fine. We hopped in the van and continued on our journey. It had been just another amusing and novel detour along the path. There would be plenty more of those to come. It was just the beginning...

Chapter 9

California or Bust

Nobody remembers with certainty what the impetus was to leave England, but it was probably the food. It might have been the weather too, or the economy, or a number of other reasons. It was obvious that Peggy was unsatisfied. For her, the romance had worn off, and she knew there was more to experience and ultimately better places to explore and to live. It had been a worthwhile experiment, but it was time to move on and try something else. One day out of the blue, I asked my mom whether we'd ever go back to America. After almost two years in England, the States seemed very far away now—like a foreign country. Mom responded with a twinkle in her eye. She said, "As a matter of fact, your father and I were just about to announce to you kids that we have decided we're moving back." We had mixed emotions. Amy and I had made many friends, but we had old friends back in New Jersey too. It would be nice to see them again and go back to our old house in Mendham. Either way seemed fine, and we were accustomed to pulling up stakes and suddenly leaving one place for the next. Before we knew it, the van was all packed up and the family was ready for the return trip across the Atlantic.

This time we didn't go on the Queen Elizabeth. We booked our passage on a smaller Polish ship called the Stefan Batore, which wasn't as elegant, and the voyage took a few days longer than the first time. The ship hit some very rough seas. The silverware in the dining galley was chained to the tables. More than once, we lost our suppers in mid-air. They always brought you more to eat, but it was like a slapstick comedy show watching the finely dressed waiters losing their balance with trays full of food. Their jackets were stained and the plates were crashing and breaking on the floor. The passengers were good-natured about it and everybody was cheering and laughing. It was a real seafaring adventure. Ron was used to being on all kinds of ships and conditions, but even he appeared a little concerned at the size of the surf and the bad weather we encountered. At any rate, we were going home and it was a thrill to be on our way.

The Stefan Batore's final destination was Montreal, Canada. It arrived on the coast of North America behind schedule and slowly made its way inland along the St. Lawrence River. We were going exceptionally slow, and there was a good reason for the delay besides the rough weather. The dock workers were on strike in Montreal and nobody would be permitted to disembark. A mob of angry picketers were blocking the unloading of passengers and cargo. As we closed in on Montreal, the ship's captain decided that they were going to try to get us off the vessel in the middle of the night. It was a secret operation. The crew were given orders to assist the willing passengers, who had been notified to be ready at a moment's notice. The Montreal police were recruited to help with security. At 3:00 a.m., Mom and Dad aroused us prematurely from our slumber and we were hushedly guided down below into the cargo section. The family all packed ourselves in the VW and waited quietly in the dark. When the moment came, we were given the signal to drive off the ship as quickly as possible. A police escort would await us and we'd be protected, but we should prepare for possible confrontation and maybe even threats or violence. Just keep driving, was the command.

The passengers were given the option of staying aboard and waiting, if they preferred, but there was no guarantee as to when the strike would end or how long we might be stuck on the ship in port. Most of the passengers were without a car. Ron and Peggy decided to take the chance and try to make the getaway as instruct-ed. At the moment of truth, Ron threw the van into gear and we escaped off the ship under the cover of night. Several police on motorcycles with flashing lights led us hurriedly away from the docks. Fortunately, the picketers were scarce at that early hour, and the evacuation was a success. Before we knew it, the family and the van were safely on the streets of Montreal. It was another case where having the camper was an advantage and a great con-venience. We had all our personal comforts with us as usual. We slithered into the darkness and immediately became part of the new surroundings like any other car in the city. Being in the VW, we felt protected as always. It was a very suspenseful adventure and a great relief to suddenly make our getaway unharmed. It was like when we had smuggled Perri across the Mexican border, or when we bolted from the London park at dawn. We were all together, and we were home free!

New Jersey wasn't that far away and we decided to hit the road immediately. Everybody had had a good rest on the sea journey, and it was time to get back to our new old home. But when we arrived at Tempe Wick Farm, things didn't work out as expected. The family who had sublet our house had suddenly fled. They had left the place a mess and Perri had disappeared too, either with or without them. That was sad news for us kids, but even sadder was the realization that we wouldn't be moving back into our house. The landlord had sold all our furniture in order to collect on the unpaid back rent. Peggy was pissed and so was the landlord. He didn't want anything to do with us anymore. Me and Amy and Julie were waiting in the car for hours while Mom and Dad argued with the owner. They were throwing their hands up and shouting. Eventually, Mom stormed back to the car. She caught her breath and then announced, "Kids, we're going to California!"

Not only were we heartbroken, now we were suddenly homeless too. We stayed in town for a few days tying up loose ends and visiting some friends, but it was a devastating blow. Our family had no place to go and we were once again living out of the van with just the clothes on our back. As our fearless leader, Peggy didn't dwell on the loss. Neither was Ron one to panic. A new opportunity had unexpectedly presented itself—a bigger dream! Mom and Dad set their sights on California, and told us to get in the car.

In 1968 in Mexico, Ron and Peggy had met some folks from California who told them all about Santa Barbara. It sounded like an ideal place with perfect weather and scenic beaches. They had been very tempted to go that year, but it was impossible at the time. Now, there was nothing to lose. Ron filled up the tank, and Peggy took out the map. They aimed for Santa Barbara and hit the road without looking back. It was April of 1975, and at least us kids got the rest of the school year off.

The van was pretty dinged up from its travels abroad. The windshield was scarred and the body was badly scratched. In England there had been plenty of snow and rain. The damp vehicle definitely needed some airing out and a good spring-cleaning and a new paint job. We spent a little money and had it painted red. That job ended up being a crappy one that barely made it to California. We got it painted again almost as soon as we arrived. It was Mom's decision to buy a small trailer that we towed behind the VW for the continental crossing. We purchased it at an RV dealer in Ohio. It was a mini-trailer that had bunk beds and a kitchenette and which provided some extra room for sleeping and to haul more stuff. Ron thought it was a bad idea, and there is a reason you never see VWs towing trailers. The van wasn't designed for such a heavy load. We were already carrying five passengers and everything we owned. There were going to be some big mountains to cross and a lot of miles. The trailer ended up being very dangerous to tow, and the van struggled from state to state. But we decided to hold onto it and see how far we got.

We weren't in any rush, however. We meandered from state to state, not going in a straight line, but seeing what there was to see along the way. From Ohio, we headed southeast to the Carolinas, where we stayed at a wonderful campsite on a very beautiful lake for a couple weeks. Mom and Dad needed some time to calm down and figure out the next steps. Gradually we started making our way westward as the weather warmed up and the summer got closer. We drove through Arkansas, Texas, Kansas, Oklahoma, Nebraska and into New Mexico, camping at every KOA along the way. We passed through the Gateway Arch at St. Louis, stopped at the Grand Canyon and the Four Corners. We almost didn't make it over the Rockies, it was such slow going. Mom and Dad told us the morbid tales of the Donner Party who were forced to eat each other one winter. As we struggled up the infamous Donner Pass, they were noticeably worried about the car, and they tried to make light of the situation by telling cannibal jokes:

"What did one cannibal say to the other?"

"I'll miss your wife—she made a great stew."

They were trying to laugh, but they were definitely nervous and stressed. This trip was different than all the others, in that it was a forced vacation we hadn't planned for. Peggy and Ron must have felt as unsure as Christopher Columbus in search of America. The unknown awaited us, and there was no turning back. Money was in short supply and the van was pushed to exhaustion. The only redeeming consolation was that we hadn't broken down yet. So, we tried to enjoy the scenery and make an adventure of it, while keeping our fingers crossed and hoping we made it to California. We never stayed in a hotel or motel once from one coast to the other. Some campsites were nice and others not so great. At a lake in one spot we literally got eaten alive by mosquitos and had to flee in the middle of the night. We crossed the planes and the mountains and the desert, seeing every kind of terrain and experiencing really good and really bad weather. Finally, we made it over the mountains and stopped at Las Vegas, but there would be no relaxing or entertainment. We spent one night in a lot behind the strip, and immediately moved on to Lake Havasu City in Arizona. That was a cheap spot and pretty nice, but it was getting very hot. I think my parents were hesitating about getting to California. Havasu is where the old London Bridge is relocated. Now it seemed like it had been a big mistake to leave England. But they remembered that they thought it had been a mistake to go there too. In Havasu, Amy and I had our eleventh birthday. We only got five dollars each and a flashlight for a present. Mom could see our disappointment and low morale, but she promised things would get better. We were moping around and acting depressed. We felt displaced, deprived, nomadic. At every new campsite, we were told to go out and make friends. What good are friends, when you're always saying goodbye?

At Lake Havasu Mom and Dad decided to ditch the mini-trailer we had reluctantly towed 2,000 miles across the country. It had only added to our burdens. It looked dorky, it was dangerous, and it was burning out the van's transmission. If they could have stuck us kids back there while on the road and towed us behind without having to listen to us cry and complain the whole way, that might have made it worth it, but that wasn't a legal option. They met a guy at the campsite who took the trailer off our hands.

My parents sold it to him when he was a bit drunk and we got the hell out of there before he changed his mind. We shed some other junk too. That was a minor relief, but it didn't solve all our problems. After we sold the trailer, I had to sleep outside and a snake slipped into my sleeping bag one night and I woke up screaming. We were worn out from weeks on the road, constantly packing up and moving on. Mom and Dad kept the faith; they knew that something better awaited us. You have to keep moving and pushing ahead, be thankful for what you have, and remain optimistic. Someday you'll appreciate it and it will make a great story. That was always the talk we got: Look how lucky you are. Your schoolmates in their cold and dreary classroom back in England would envy you, seeing the Grand Canyon, soaking up the hot desert sun, on holiday, and free as birds! What's wrong with you? Cheer up.

We left Lake Havasu and it only got hotter. The desert kept going and going with no sign of shade or relief from the heat. Why can't it rain every day, like in England? Dad laughed. "You just can't win with you kids, can you?" Finally...we were out of the desert. Everything changed and the scenery appeared to suddenly open up like a golden treasure. Could it be true? Had we finally arrived? On a beautiful June morning in 1975, we saw the majestic California coast for the first time. It looked like an unbelievable dream. We had made it.

"Get out of the car, kids. We're here!"

Chapter 10

Paradise Found

It was a big reward to stay at a motel on the beach when we finally landed in Santa Barbara. The Sea Breeze Leisure Lodge was our temporary home for a week or two. We couldn't keep that up for long. Ron and Peggy immediately fell in love with Santa Barbara and there was no question they wanted to stay. I was really homesick for England. I stayed in bed and refused to go outside. I believed that if I closed my eyes for long enough, when I opened them, I would be back at our house on the Thames. That didn't work obviously. Eventually, some other kids at the motel coaxed me outside and my attitude improved a little. Homesickness can be very debilitating. It's like the child's version of depression. The best remedy is to get outside, but I was always outside. How many times do I remember my parents telling us kids they didn't want to see us until dinner time. "Go find something to do. You've got the whole world out there!" They shamed me. They said I was acting like an old man confined to a nursing home. Whenever television was available, that's all I wanted to do. Both our parents had grown up in the days before TV, and even though they allowed it, they thought it was frying our brains. We sat with our noses two inches from the screen for hours on end. My parents just shook their heads. To me, it seemed like I had spent half my life in campsites, and now I was compensating for all the shows I had missed. The truth is all of our generation were television junkies. Fortunately, as I got older, the early influences of my parents rubbed off. My dad was a good role model in the long run. He never succumbed to the temptations of the modern world, all the consumerism and materialism and junky food. He seemed like a pretty boring person, but now I understand that he had the right idea. The older I get, the more I see that I am turning into him. Your parents have a big effect on how you turn out, even if you rebel at first or don't see it right away.

Santa Barbara was very expensive. Honestly, it was out of our league. We couldn't find an affordable place to live, so we did what we had always done: we camped and we traveled around. I want to use a different word than "camped" or "camped out," as it implies a kind of transiency and instability—as in, we camped because we didn't have a real roof over our heads—which is what I've just basically admitted to. On the other hand, if you choose to camp, if you elect to sleep in a tent...well then, that sounds more romantic. The lifestyle we'd had until that time was a fine line between these two perspectives. My parents managed to convince us that "roughing it" was what made life rewarding, and they were right about that; I also felt that they were totally conning us at times, but what choice did we have?

Let's face it, we didn't always camp because it was fun. We were living on a shoe string, but Mom always knew how much we had and kept to a strict budget. When it came to the sacrifices one had to make in order to be comfortably middle-class, like working all the time, or signing into a long-term mortgage, my parents were simply not willing to do that. They were intelligent enough to be aware of the serious and consequential trade-off between a life of security and a life of freedom, and they purposely chose the latter. Of course, most people want to be able to collect the benefits of both worlds, and we did our best too. Sooner or later, you have to decide what is more important. It's a crucial and existential decision we all must face, and the one which ultimately determines your happiness and self-respect. Really, it is the only question there is.

We spent the whole first summer in California touring the Golden State. We visited every place from Big Sur to Yosemite to the Sierras to San Diego, camping up and down the coast and zigzagging through the deserts and mountains and valleys. There was so much to see. Us kids had been out of school for months, so there was nothing to tie the family down. The previous summer, when we had camped in France and Spain, we at least had our house in England to return to. It was different this time; we were essentially homeless, but that fact didn't seem to bother my parents. We had time to travel up to Oregon and Washington and added the west coast states to our resume. By this point, the camper had been to all the eastern U.S. states, all the southern ones, and now the western states were checked off the list. The van had been in seven countries, and it was only three years old. Amy and I had just turned eleven, Julie was almost ten, Mom was already forty-five, and Dad had passed the sixty mark.

As the summer drew to a close, we came back to Santa Barbara and Peggy started pounding the pavement again looking for our next permanent home. She was tenacious as always. She went up and down every street poking her head in the windows of any place that looked available. It pissed her off that the realtors in Santa Barbara had such a strangle-hold on the market. They would rather a house remain empty than lower the price. Even in 1975, to buy a house in Santa Barbara had become impossible for most regular folks, and for us especially. Peggy eventually stumbled upon a small place that was empty. It had been for sale for a year but with no takers. Mom convinced the realtor to rent it to us until it sold. The agent agreed but wanted to be able to show the house on the weekends. At a pretty good rent we moved in, and it looked as though we were all settled for the start of the school year. However, the very next Saturday a buyer made an offer, and the house was sold right from under us. It was a big disappointment.

Ron and Peggy thought seriously about going back to San Miguel in Mexico. It was a place they knew they could afford, but what about school? Things were looking desperate. There were thirty days until escrow closed to find another place—any place. They decided they'd just have to bite the bullet and somehow manage to pay the high rents that were expected. That meant digging into the measly savings they had, but there was no other choice. For $275 per month, we moved into a small two-bedroom house in September of 1975. Mom made sure there was a safe place to park the van off the street, which she always insisted on. It may not sound like a lot of money now, but it was a crazy amount in those days. Mom and Dad would have to sleep in the living room, and we'd be eating a lot of corned beef hash. But it was better than a tent—at least from us kids' point of view. In the meantime, Mom would keep looking for a better place and we'd make it work. Welcome to Paradise!

Chapter 11

Happy Nest

In the winter of 1977, we headed down to Mexico for a short trip to Guaymas on the Sea of Cortez. We celebrated another Christmas camping on the beach like we had done in Florida. On the drive down, just before crossing the border near Mexicali, the van's odometer turned over at 100,000 miles, and started at zero again. Mom and Dad thought that was the coolest thing in the world! But the car was tired. It needed a new engine, and after having taken us to so many distant places, it certainly deserved one. We needed a lot of other things too. Since we had moved to Santa Barbara, the family was living leaner than usual. At some point, you have to decide what your priorities are. Dad loved Santa Barbara. He had found the perfect place to enjoy retirement on a budget and he encouraged the rest of us to be grateful for how good we had it. He was tan and fit and enjoyed swimming in the ocean every day. Mom also rebelled against the work-a-day world. Sure, it was hard not to envy the rich people living in big houses with swimming pools who surrounded us everywhere, but they had their problems too. We had no reason to complain.

Nonetheless, the U.S. economy was in poor condition. Inflation was out of control. The price of fuel was going through the roof and there were lines at gas stations that went around the block. Amy had just gotten braces, and then Ron broke his hip when he fell off his bicycle. On top of all that, we got news that come summer, we'd have to move out of our house. It was the most difficult time we had faced, but really it was nothing new. If worse came to worse, we'd end up camping again. Whatever money there was had to go into re-building the van's motor. After all, the VW might end up being our home again soon. Peggy knew that as long as she took care of the van, it would take care of us. It would keep the family together, and we'd get through the hard times. But we were running out of time and things were looking pretty desperate. The thought of having to live at the local campsite was tragic for Amy and me, but Mom said that school would be out by then, so what difference would it make? "Everybody goes camping at the beach in the summer. It's fun."

"They go because they want to—not because they have to," Amy argued. "It's so embarrassing."

But Mom said nobody would know. "Don't be silly."

As things turned out, it never got to that point. Our luck turned around and a miracle happened at the last minute. It wasn't a miracle at all, actually; it was Mom's perseverance and hard work that saved us as usual. She found us a better house—a bigger house that we loved with plenty of room for everybody. We would have to rent out one of the extra bedrooms and fix the place up, but it would work and we'd survive just fine. In fact, we'd be much better off. We moved in that summer and our troubles were over. To celebrate the good fortune, our family car got the rebuilt engine it was owed, along with a brand-new coat of paint—an easy cream color now. Life was looking up!

Looking back, I think Mom got an unusual thrill from these periods of uncertainty and insecurity. It was almost as if she invited them; as if she was testing fate—or testing her own faith. If I didn't know better, I'd even say she planned them—as crazy as that sounds. Inevitably, we'd find ourselves in a challenging or precarious situation—on the verge of homelessness—and then we'd get suddenly rescued by an unforeseen opportunity. Most people spend their whole lives evading these kinds of predicaments. Who the hell would embrace insecurity? But just like anything you fear, it's better to face it and then you find out it's not as bad as you thought. Even fifty years later, I still have the same van to rely on. I worry about the future like anybody else, but I assure myself that as bad as things get I can always live in the VW—and I'd have a lot more room than we did in the old days! I think that deep down people secretly cherish that kind of existential risk. You have to hit rock-bottom sometimes, to really bounce back. You have to die to really live. Mom wasn't reckless; to the contrary, she was always well-prepared and resourceful. But unlike most people, she wasn't afraid to cast caution to the wind when it really mattered. She wasn't afraid to be vulnerable, because she knew she was strong and that life always provided you with what you truly need to be happy and fulfilled in the end. She had proven it to herself time and time again That's how she felt about her van too, and that's the legacy she left us with.

For the next few years, we continued to make holiday trips in the revived camper. Mom insisted on driving everywhere while we were still all together as a family. Oceans and mountains and deserts never stopped her. We could have all boarded an airplane and accomplished in a few short hours what took days and weeks on the road, but she wanted those wheels beneath her. From the camper, you witnessed every mile first-hand, and you saw the scenery evolve and transpire and blossom and change, and it was all connected in one long stream. Seeing the world from a moving car created profound emotions that were always changing. You suddenly felt sad driving through places that looked lonely or desolate, imagining the lives of the people who were stuck there or who had no desire to leave. But not us. We were always off to explore newer, better, more exciting places. We could go wherever we wanted. We had wheels, we had mobility, we were free!

I remember many times as a kid returning home in the van from a long trip late at night. I climbed into the cozy niche behind the back seat. That was my spot when I wanted to be totally alone. In that quiet compartment I never cared where I was, as long as we kept moving. The longer and farther we drove, the safer I felt. If we had careened off the side of a mountain, that would have been fine with me. What a serene and perfect way to go. It was so soothing back there in the dark, in my one-man space capsule, shooting through the infinite universe. I wasn't aware of the passing landscape. I only glimpsed the tops of the trees and flashes of light and darting shadows that grew and subsided in the night. I felt the turns and the jerky stops, the car slowing down and speeding up. I could feel the shifting of the gears and the thrill of acceleration and coasting down long hills. I didn't want it to ever stop. I just wanted to keep moving forever and ever...peacefully...and never arriving.

It seems to me that every member of our family lived in their own private world too. Dad pondered life from his silent realm.

Julie was somewhere far away. Amy had her secret fantasies and schemes. Mom was always making grand and covert plans. We drove for miles and miles without communicating, looking out the window and imagining and dreaming. We were a ship of introverts, rarely feeling the need to share our thoughts with one another. Yet we were one as a family, driving in the same car, all going to the same places together. Every family is unique, and a little weird. Was it a karmic arrangement our individual souls had chosen, a pact to help us on our cosmic journey through life and the beyond? I never thought about it back then, but now it's very clear. Why were we all here in the same place, in the same car, going who knows where? What did we have in common? We were pulled in closely, not by deep love or effusive feelings, but by a gravitational and elliptical force that seemed to guide each of us distinctly. It was a force that held us all together like atoms in a molecule.

By the early eighties, the counterculture lifestyle was losing its appeal for a lot of Americans, especially in California. The Baby Boomers were aging and settling down. Hippies were turning into yuppies. It happened pretty fast. But never for a single moment did Peggy ever consider getting rid of the van. She was never a hippy anyway, and she never got lured in by the desire to be like everyone else. During all those years, they never bought another car. Whether the van kept up with the times or not was irrelevant. It would take a few more decades, but eventually touring around in a VW camper became cool again. As long as it continued to carry the family, it fulfilled its purpose. There is no question that Peggy's van gave her life meaning and joy. Year after year, the bond grew stronger until she and the car had become one and the same. They were conjoined at the hip and inseparable. Like a centaur, they were a single creature, mythical and divine.

Sadly, us kids would not be part of the van-life for much longer. We'd have to make our own way in the world. Amy and I entered high school, and the last thing we wanted was to be associated with, let alone dropped off in public, by parents who drove an old Scooby van. Mom and Dad would keep going and keep doing what they had done. Peggy would never stop, and Ron was always at her side, along for the ride. The nest was going to be empty soon, but the van was still full of dreams and ready to roll—as it always had been.

Chapter 12

Snowbirds

In June of 1982, Amy and I graduated from high school. My parents had helped me buy my own first used car a few months earlier. I didn't need a car; it was their idea. I soon realized it was all part of a big plan. It wasn't my plan—because I didn't have one. I wasn't motivated to go to college or do anything. I was working a measly part-time job at an ice cream parlor, and I was spending most of my time hanging out and partying with my friends. I needed a good kick in the pants. Mom had always warned us that once we turned eighteen, we were on our own, so it wasn't a real shocker when I got kicked out of the house a couple months after graduation. Mom probably expected it to be a first warning, and when I came back with my tail between my legs there would be room for negotiation. But I got a lucky break. I never came home, and I made the transition very quickly on my own. I packed all my stuff into my car and drove away into adulthood and never looked back. Amy was next. They did their best to set her in the right direction. She started working full-time and taking classes and was able to move out and get a roommate. It sounds a little cruel, but that's how it was in those days. The job of the parents is to prepare you for life on your own, and we had to grow up fast.

The big question was what they were going to do with Julie. As an adult, she would never be able to take care of herself. Compared to her, Amy and I didn't need any special treatment or sympathy; we were as able-bodied as any other eighteen-year-old with a high school diploma. But Julie was helpless on her own. Of course, Mom and Dad were well-aware of that; they couldn't just kick her out too. To continue to care for her, however, was only going to get harder and harder. Dad was almost seventy. Even though she was severely handicapped, Julie was becoming a young adult too, and she deserved to have a life of her own like anybody else. Mom and Dad would make sure she got the love and care she needed, but they didn't have a solution yet. Peggy took on the challenge as she always did. She was always one to plan things far in advance, and obviously this was something she'd been working on for a long time. As nice as California was, the state didn't provide the kind of resources Julie needed as an adult, and Mom and Dad didn't have all the resources either. The answer was in Canada. All of us kids were Canadian citizens based on our father's status as a British-Canadian. We had been born in the U.S., but we were awarded dual citizenship when we turned eighteen. It was a very generous offer from the Canadians. Normally, you'd have to renounce one nationality in favor of the other, but in our case, we were able to retain both. There were other benefits for Ron and Peggy as well, if they lived in Canada. So, it was settled. In the spring of 1984, they packed up the van and said goodbye to Santa Barbara.

Of course, Julie went with them. They strapped her into her seatbelt in the back seat as they had done a million times before and headed north on the 101. Their destination was Victoria, British Columbia. Being the astute person she was, Julie sensed that something was different. She looked up from her book more frequently than usual and seemed curiously aware that they weren't coming back. She didn't appear to object or resist. She was used to long drives and new adventures in the van. She could hear her parents' discussions in the cockpit, and there was no reason to think she didn't know what was going on. Eventually, she must have figured it all out: This trip was about her. It was the beginning of Julie's brand-new life as a young woman. It must have been very exciting for her.

It took a lot of time and hard work to find a good place for Julie in Victoria. Mom and Dad also had to situate themselves. After months of perseverance, they were able to secure an ideal spot for Julie. She moved into a regular three-bedroom house with two or three other residents that were mentally handicapped like her. There was a staff of caregivers who worked shifts around the clock to take care of them. They provided Julie with a nice environment which was very normal and comfortable. She'd continue attending school every day and do activities and go on field trips, etc. Best of all, it was a program that would be paid for by the Canadian government indefinitely. That was really a huge relief that put everybody at great ease. As always, Peggy hadn't settled for anything less than she knew Julie deserved. Finally, she was satisfied. Julie fit right into her new home and appeared very pleased. For the first time in her life, she was independent from her family. She was her own person. Mom and Dad could see her as often as they'd like. They could take her out of town on trips. They would always be nearby.

Peggy went through the exact same process of locating a place for herself and Dad. It took a while as usual, with a lot of pavement-pounding and knocking on doors. Within a year, she finally found a small place for them that was right on the sea. From their front window they looked across the Juan de Fuca Strait, at the peaks of the Olympic mountains in the distance. Like their home on the Thames in England, they were on the water again. That pleased Ron. As usual, Peggy had not accepted anything less. She kept searching and searching, until she found the perfect spot. That was her talent. All the kids were out of the nest; the hardest work was behind them. Now, the couple could really hit the road and have some fun!

British Columbia in the summertime is as nice as Santa Barbara, but the winters get dark and cold and rainy. Sometimes it even snows. Eventually, they got the itch to make a return visit to a place they had always loved, San Miguel de Allende. In the winter of '87, they took off down the coast. Julie was happy to see her parents off, and they promised to be back soon. They drove south through Santa Barbara and crossed the border in Tijuana and kept going down the Baja until they reached the peninsula's southernmost tip. From La Paz, there was a ferry to the mainland at Mazatlan. They boarded the ferry with the van, and the next morning arrived in old familiar territory. From Mazatlan, they climbed inland to Guadalajara, then continued east all the way to Guanajuato. It was a road they had been on fifteen years earlier, but they were going in the opposite direction this time, and without Perri or the kids. All the memories of those good times with the family came flooding back. It was enchanting to be in Mexico again, and they raced to make it to San Miguel de Allende for a long-awaited homecoming. Peggy went through the exact process of persistent house searching to find them a place to live in San Miguel. Eventually, they were able to spend their summers in Victoria and the winters in Mexico. They found a small house that needed a lot of work, but once it was fixed up it became their home for many years. The rent was cheap enough that they could afford to lock up the place during the vacant months, and return every winter. They finally had created the lifestyle they had always dreamed of. It was perfect. It was heaven.

The long trek was well over two-thousand miles from the west coast of Canada to central Mexico. For the next fifteen winters they did that drive every year, there and back, in the same sturdy van, right on schedule. One year, after they had driven all the way down the Baja, they discovered that the ferry had been suddenly canceled. They had to turn around and drive the whole way back up the Baja and re-enter Mexico at the Arizona border and head down along the mainland. That unforeseen mishap cost them several thousand miles and a week's worth of driving. The Baja highway was notorious for its dangerous conditions and bad weather. They didn't repeat that mistake again. Thereafter, they established a better route from California to Yuma and then across the border at Nogales, and down the coast of the Sea of Cortez through Navajoa and then to Mazatlan. The annual migration put a lot of miles on the van, but Peggy insisted on driving every year. The couple and the car showed no signs of quitting; in fact, it energized them and rejuvenated them. It was worth it to get away from the Canadian winters, and before heading back they drove to the beach and spent a couple more weeks soaking up the Mexican sun. They always stayed at the same motel in a small town called Guayabitos in Nayarit. When it was finally time to leave Mexico, they headed north again, back through Arizona, California, Oregon, and Washington, to Canada, just in time for spring.

Chapter 13

Keepin' On

Peggy had every leg of the trek memorized and always knew what to expect. She knew exactly where the gas stations were and logged every mile in a handy notebook. She told me the drive cost about $500 each way in gas and lodging and toll roads. That was back when it cost about thirty bucks to fill the tank (14 gallons). It was about the same price as two airline tickets would have cost, but they never thought twice about taking the van. They stopped in Santa Barbara for several days along the way and stayed a couple nights at the beach in Guaymas or Mazatlan. A normal day of driving was five or six hours. A comfortable speed for the van was about 65 m.p.h., and they completed about three hundred miles a day. With Ron as her co-pilot, the two made a good team. Ron was sixteen years older than Peggy, but each of them was still driving well into their late eighties. Every once in a while, one of them might retire into the rear cabin for a short nap, but that was rare. Peggy was fueled by regular breaks of instant coffee. She had a traveling kettle that plugged into the car. As long of a trip as it was, the driving was comfortable and relaxing for the most part. Escaping the northwest, they might hit rain or cold weather for the first few days, but once they crossed the border and got down into Mexico, it was nice and warm. The only long day they had was driving non-stop from Mazatlan to San Miguel. That took a good twelve hours, but then it was done. They had the next several months to relax and enjoy their second home in beautiful Mexico. Best of all, they had the van with them to use every day.

They brought all the things they needed that you couldn't get in Mexico. It was the same story every time: Peggy over-packed the van and Ron complained. But she said that if he didn't have his crumpets and tea at exactly four o'clock, or his special assortment of cheeses, he got grumpy and out of sorts. He was the typical Englishman in that respect. No matter where one finds oneself, in whatever inhospitable or uncivilized conditions, one must always insist upon a respectable and timely cup of tea with all the appropriate accouterments. There could be a storm blowing the roof off, but Ron always kept calm and carried on. You've got to appreciate the power of a simple hot beverage to provide that kind of composure and stability. That is what the British are famous for, after all. Without Peggy, however, Ron wouldn't have been able to keep it together. He left everything up to her.

The trip became a yearly routine they had practically perfected. However, there was always the chance of car trouble along the way. Often, the best part of traveling were the surprises and the discoveries they never expected. For Peggy at least, the risks of taking the van made the trip more exciting and adventurous. Even if they broke down in the middle of nowhere, they had all the comforts of home with them. They were always prepared, but they enjoyed plenty of spontaneity as well. Whatever happened, good or bad, it would all be in the rearview mirror soon enough. If you worry about the things that might go wrong, you'll never leave the house. Besides, the VW had proven itself to be very dependable year after year. They knew they could count on it.

One year, after spending the winter in San Miguel, they headed to the beach as usual. This time they decided to try a different route, which took them over a big volcano. It was a steep climb. The car started to sputter and gasp, and the engine failed just as they reached the top of the pass. There was nobody around and no cars on the road. All they could do was throw her into neutral and coast down the mountain as far as they could, hoping they'd spot some help before the car finally stopped. They ended up coasting twenty miles without the engine, enjoying the scenery and the free ride, but fearing the moment it would all come to a slow end. Down, down, down they went…quiet as a butterfly. At the very bottom of the giant hill was a tiny village with an old country inn. It looked actually quite charming. They managed to coast right up to the front of the hotel…inch by inch…before the car could finally roll no farther. Well, fate had delivered them here, and what choice had they but to check in for the night? They needed a rest and to take a good look at the map, anyway.

As it turns out, there was a garage down the street. They found the mechanic who walked over and easily fixed the car. He got them on the road again the very next morning, and they continued on their merry way. The detour had turned out to be a substantial shortcut that saved them time and money. After that, they were always willing to try a new route. When in doubt, they always took a chance. What's the worst thing that could happen? Sometimes they got lost or had to backtrack, but other times they discovered really cool new places. If the VW got into trouble, somebody always knew how to fix it, and it was never expensive in Mexico. Delays and detours were all part of the adventure, and they made great stories.

In 1991, I went to Guadalajara to study Spanish. I ended up staying there for a couple years and becoming an English teacher. I used to visit my parents in San Miguel regularly or they'd stop and see me for a few days on their way to or from San Miguel. Once, I took a bus ride to Toluca near Mexico City to do some sightseeing. It was about an eight-hour trip. The bus stopped half-way for lunch in the desert at a roadside cafe. I was eating my tacos and I looked out the window and saw my parents' van whiz by. What the hell! It was their car for sure, I'd recognize it anywhere. I shouted, "Hey! That's my parents!" but there was nothing I could do. I called them a few days later and told them I thought I saw the VW on the highway, and Mom said, "Yes, that was us. We were picking up some friends at the airport in Leon." What a trip that was!

The van was like an amiable and carefree traveler, whose home was wherever it hung its hat. It seemed to fit in and be welcomed everywhere, by friends and strangers alike. Good fortune and luck followed it no matter where it went. It has always had and still has a warm and friendly personality that people like. I know it's just a car, but it has a smile on its face and goodness in its heart. I think most of that comes from the love and care my parents had for the van, especially my mother. She's a good car, Ma!

Chapter 14

Papa

In 2000, after a decade and a half, Ron and Peggy gave up their winter home in San Miguel de Allende. They packed up their belongings and shuttered the doors of their little casita for the last time. Certainly, they were sad, but there was plenty else to see and to discover, and the memories they had could never be taken away. They left the house in Canada as well and decided to settle for a happy medium. They moved back to Santa Barbara, and did something they had never done: they bought a house. Actually, it was a modest mobile home located in Carpinteria, not far from where Amy and I and our children all lived. Let's face it, Peggy and Ron were never going to settle down, and that's as close as they ever got. They still kept driving to Canada and Mexico for regular visits. They went to Alberta and Ottawa and explored the landmarks of the Old Wild West, and drove through the scenic Copper Canyon and the Sierra Madre mountains. They visited Vera Cruz on the Gulf of Mexico.

Julie was alone in Victoria now, but Mom and Dad continued to drive up and see her every year. The staff where she lived said that as the fall approached, Julie would stand at the front window and look out for her parents. Never disappointing her, they inevitably showed up in the familiar van. She had been in the same house for fifteen years now, and she had a satisfying life of her own. She seemed to be very happy as a full-time Canadian. A few times she flew down to Santa Barbara for a week or two, accompanied by one of her caregivers. Julie was an aunt now and Peggy and Ron were the grandparents of three. We would all pack into the van and go out to dinner at our favorite restaurant. Our cousins from England and Ron's sister came for regular visits too. The VW was always at the center of these memorable family reunions. Finally, we'd all say goodbye, and Mom and Dad would putter away, with a honk and a wave. The next time we saw them it was always the friendly old VW you spotted or heard first. The recognizable and bouncy ring of its engine was unmistakable. It was always a reassuring sign that nothing had changed.

They continued to maintain the van and keep her in top shape. Whatever the car needed it got. That included a new transmission and another fresh coat of paint or two. Mom had it done a khaki color for a few years, but that wasn't quite warm enough for her liking. On a visit back to San Miguel, they invested some real money for the best paint job the car ever got. It was in the shop for almost two weeks. The crew took the whole body apart, fender by fender, and really did a primo job. The color was a soft mocha tone now. With its white upper body, the van looked like a soothing cup of cappuccino—with foam on top. I was with Mom and Dad when they picked up the car from the shop. It cost about $1,000, which is no small amount in Mexican pesos. That was the last paint job the car has ever needed. The quality of the paint used in Mexico seemed better, having something to do with the lead it contained. Since 2005, it has lasted very nicely and still looks like new. By this time, the odometer had turned over three more times, and it eventually got another rebuild.

Unfortunately, Ron was getting pretty old himself, and unlike the van, his parts couldn't be replaced forever. He was well into his nineties by this point. Nonetheless, he continued to swim in the ocean every day and Mom's great cooking kept him as healthy as could be. He was very regimented from a life in the navy and very disciplined. He got up at daybreak every morning to do his calisthenics before anybody else was awake. He always took cold showers too. That was the key to his health and longevity. He continued painting his watercolors and taking art classes, and his mind was alert and he never lost his wits. But there's only so far a person can go, even with a lifestyle as nourishing and rewarding as his. In 2007, the couple made the usual drive down to Mexico for a stay at the beach. Dad was showing signs of fatigue and he had lost weight. He seemed to be losing that vigor for life he had always displayed. Mom was doing all the driving by now. The truth is, she was sixteen years younger than he was, and she probably pushed him farther than he was capable at the very end. That was just her nature, to refuse to give up and to keep going no matter what. He'd had a great life and a long life, but it was finally time for him to bow out. In November of 2008, Captain Ron completed his final voyage. He was just two months short of his 95th birthday. He'd been around the world three times, not including all the miles in the camper. He was married to Peggy for forty-five years—pretty good, considering he didn't get hitched until he was fifty. He had Mom to thank for the best years of his life. Ronald Snowden Hurst was born in 1914 in Yorkshire, England. His ashes were scattered at sea by the Royal Canadian Navy. Hail and farewell, Papa.

Chapter 15

The Boss

It was only a month after Ron's death, but Mom insisted on making the annual drive to Guayabitos by herself. What else was she going to do? She had no intention of quitting her lifestyle, and showed absolutely no signs of slowing down. I had a couple weeks off for Christmas and I wanted to go with her in Dad's place. I had visited my parents dozens of times in Mexico but I had always flown. I was hesitant about driving the car such a long distance, but I thought if Mom can do it, there's no reason why I can't too. We were going to drive to San Miguel first, and then down to the beach after that. I'd fly home from Puerto Vallarta and Mom would stay for another month on her own.

We left a few days before Christmas. Believe it or not—I had never driven the van before in my life. When I was a little kid, Mom would sit me on her lap in the driver's seat and let me shift the gears. It was the same car, just a few decades later. I was a little intimidated at first. Mom agreed to let me take turns with her, but she insisted on doing most of the driving. She knew the route by heart, and I just did as she told me. Along the way, she pointed out all the landmarks and told me stories of past trips and the unexpected twists and turns they had experienced over the years. The van was in great shape and we didn't encounter any trouble or surprises the whole way. We drove the regular route and kept right on schedule. Our first night was in a motel in Yuma, and then we drove through the Arizona desert to the border at Nogales, where we spent the second night. The next morning it was snowing. We had to get the car's paperwork processed before entering Mexico. Mom told me the Mexican authorities always jerked her around a bit just to show who's boss, but the line was relatively short and we were able to get into Mexico and on our way nice and early.

Over the course of the third day, we gradually acclimated to the foreign landscape of Mexico. Slowly you get used to being there, and the culture shock isn't so sudden. For a whole day you go through the Sonoran desert, which is pretty bleak and unfriendly. The road signs change to kilometers. The towns get smaller and smaller and finally disappear. The radio stations go from English to Spanish to nothing at all. It's a lonely and forgotten place. You can't help but think about death—which is comforting to the Mexicans for some reason. I fell asleep while Mom was driving, and when I woke up we were going through an old town that was all in miniature. The churches were tiny, all the buildings were tiny, the walls, the statues. It was totally empty. I thought I was still dreaming. Then I realized that it wasn't a town; it was a cemetery.

After the desert, the scenery started to fill in and get greener with every mile. I started feeling really happy and optimistic. I think we had passed the halfway mark by now, and I remembered that we were on our way to a beautiful place. The panorama expanded and brightly filled the front wind screen like a larger-than-life movie. We were gulping up the miles and going full-speed ahead. It was just like the old days. Not since I was a young teenager had I been on a road trip in the family van. I was in my forties now. Time had slipped away so suddenly, but it was all coming back: the same car, the same feelings, the same spirit of adventure. It felt like Dad was still with us. I was in his seat now, but he was there over my shoulder. I realized how much I missed the excitement of traveling by car and going to the places we loved and to newer places, chasing the road of life and being totally free. I was really glad to be driving with Mom and carrying on the tradition. It was an awesome feeling.

At the end of the day, we pulled into the El Mayo motel in Navojoa. I made a joke about checking into the Mayo. It felt great to arrive safely at a place that was so welcoming and peaceful. I had never been there, myself, but Mom told me it was a place she and Dad loved. The rooms were all arranged around an interior courtyard that was closed off from the street. We parked the VW right in front of the room and unloaded the things we needed for the night. The owners asked about Dad, and Mom told them that he had passed away the month before. They said nice things about my old man, and Mom introduced me. Even though she didn't speak Spanish much, she could get by pretty good. I think it made her proud that I spoke Spanish. It was because of her and Dad, after all, that I had been exposed to the language at a young age and went on to study it and to love Mexico as much as they did. I had lived in Mexico and visited many times on my own, so I felt somewhat useful that I was able to translate here and there, but Mom was very capable on her own.

The next morning we hit the road at 8 a.m. "I'll drive," she said. There was a tricky section of busy traffic, ramps, and bridges to get through, but she knew exactly what to do. Once out of town, she let me take the wheel and the scenery became absolutely beautiful and the weather was as pleasant as could be. It was all agricultural farmland that stretched for miles in every direction. I realized how much I had been missing all those years by not driving to Mexico, through all the countryside. I never understood why my parents had always insisted on taking the van. It was so much easier to hop on a plane and just get there in a couple hours. Now, I understood why. Whatever we needed we had with us. We didn't have to share our space with strangers or follow anybody's orders or schedules.

By the fourth day, there suddenly seemed to be an awful lot of toll roads. Every twenty minutes, we had to slow down for another one. Mom was prepared as always. She had a purse full of pesos stashed under the back seat. She told me where to find it, and she had enough small bills and coins to cover the exact change at every gate. As vehicles approached the toll booths, there were signs that warned: "Vibradores a 50 metros." Gnarly speed bumps rattled the car's suspension. When the drivers slowed down and prepared to stop, a little swarm of local vendors with baskets of food ran up to the cars selling tamales and drinks and other snacks. But they never had any vibrators, and we never asked.

The last leg of the trip was a long stretch of palm trees for miles and miles. We were almost there. We made a final stop for gas in Culiacan, three hours north of Mazatlan, where we planned to take a break for a few days at the beach. At the gas station, Mom tried to open the sliding door to sit in back and have some coffee, but it wouldn't open. We tried everything and it wouldn't budge.

We'd still be able to drive fine but eventually when it came to unloading the van, it was going to be a real problem. In the whole history of the car, that had never happened before.

Finally, we reached Mazatlan right before sundown. I couldn't wait to check into the Belmar and throw on my swim trunks and jump into the warm ocean. I had been there many times on my own and I still go every year at Christmas time. Even though it had been snowing in Nogales two days earlier, by now it was pretty hot and sticky. We rolled into town, but instead of heading straight to the hotel on the beach, Mom suddenly turned in the wrong direction. I said, "Where are you going, Mom?" She told me she knew a mechanic in town and she wanted to have him take a look at the door. "Now?" I groaned. "Why now? It's Christmas eve." She wasn't tired at all. She said it would just take a minute and she drove up and down the streets in an old industrial part of town, trying to remember where it was. Finally, we found the shop but it was closed. She went knocking on the door and nobody answered. She kept knocking. She said, "I hear music." An old guy answered the door and he had a big smile. "Hola, Peggy! Feliz NaviDad!" He sure seemed friendly. I was so impatient, probably just like Dad had been; I really needed to get in that ocean before the sun set. Mom started chatting with him and told him about the car door not working. He laughed and said, "I'm already drunk, Peggy. Can you back tomorrow?" *Thank God*, I thought. We made it to the Hotel Belmar just in time to get my swim. That night we had to pull some bags out the back hatch of the van to take up to the room. But the next day (which was Christmas), the sliding door opened fine, and ever since then it never happened again.

We stayed at the beach in Mazatlan for three relaxing days, and then Mom drove us all the way to San Miguel in twelve hours. That was a long drive, but she didn't want to stop in Guadalajara. She had found it was better to keep going and she drove like the devil. The last stretch was very dark and the road was narrow and winding back and forth. That was the first time I was aware of a kind of obsession within her. I remembered when I was a kid, terrified and clinging to the car floor, afraid to look out the window. The road wasn't as bad now as it had been in those days, but Mom was driven as ever. Maybe she was trying not to think about Dad, or the past. She had to keep going. She had to try harder than ever now. I let her do what she had to do. I held on tight, and we got there. We checked into a modest pension near the center called *The Guest*. It was sad that my parents didn't have their nice little house anymore, and Dad was gone now too. But I had so many great memories there, going back to when I was just a kid, and even before. It was a bittersweet experience. Mom still had plenty of friends in town. They all talked about what a nice guy Dad had been. One of them told me, "You're the man of the family now." I secretly thought: *No. Mom's still the man of the family*. That was the truth.

We stayed almost a week, and then drove down to Guayabitos on the coast. We went through the agave plantations covering all the hills and it was a leisurely downhill coast all the way. We got there easily in a day. The car had run perfectly the whole trip. It was so relaxing and fun. I wondered why driving in my own vehicles had always seemed to stress me out so much. The VW had a generous spirit that I could genuinely feel. I had total trust in her, I knew she had our back. On this trip Mom was passing on to me that sacred experience, that special relationship, and now I knew how it felt. I understood what she had always known, and why she kept driving and kept going.

After a short stay at the beach, I flew back to California. Sitting in the airplane I thought about the drive down, everything we had seen, all the dusty little towns we passed through and the terrain we covered, the hours and hours we had spent looking ahead and breathing in the scenery, talking about Dad and Mexico and all the people we had met and revisited. In a few weeks, Mom would be driving back the way we had come. She'd be doing it alone, but I wasn't worried. She had herself. She had the van. I knew she was the boss, and I wasn't worried one bit.

Chapter 16
Operation Rescue

In 2010, Peggy made her usual trip to Canada in September to see Julie. The weather was still very hot on the drive up, going through northern California, Oregon, and Washington. That made for really unpleasant driving. The engine got pushed to the extremes, but Mom made it in two days. She spent a week in B.C. at her usual spot, a little motel north of Victoria in the woods next to one of the beautiful lakes up there. She picked up her daughter every day and took her for a drive in the family van, which Julie was so accustomed to and always felt at home in. They visited a popular beach in town where Dad had loved to go. She dressed Julie in her bathing suit and they both had a swim and a picnic out of the car. She had some big new fashion catalogs that Julie enthusiastically ate up, though she barely touched her food.

Julie did love her coffee, though; she rarely had anything else. She was as skinny as Dad was, but she was a survivor too. McDonald's was her favorite place to sit and sip. Mom was a big fan of coffee too. Julie liked to be inside the restaurant and around people. Although she never talked, you could tell how much she enjoyed being there and soaking it all in. Mom had to cut her off from the caffeine, she always wanted more. Julie let Mom know when she was done and wanted to leave. She'd stand up abruptly and start moving toward the door impatiently, pointing and making her intentions clear, voicing her opinion with noises that Mom understood. After the outing, Julie wanted to get back home and be by herself. She pushed Mom out of the house with an insistence that signaled, "I'll see you later. Come back tomorrow if you want." You couldn't call Julie or make plans with her on the telephone. There were a few occasions when Mom went over there to pick her up and Julie refused to budge. She was stubborn, even with her old Mom. She literally stood her ground, and you couldn't move her outside or into the van. Sometimes she got upset, but once she was in her familiar spot in the backseat with her book, she stopped complaining and went along. Finally, Mom said goodbye to Julie until the next fall, and so it went, year after year. Same Mom, same van, same coffee. It was a big circle. Peggy got on the road again and raced back to Santa Barbara.

That January, Peggy turned eighty years old. The van was still a sprite and sexy thirty-eight. Together they continued to make the winter trip from California to Mexico every year after Christmas. Unfortunately, Peggy's health started to suffer. She had to be hospitalized suddenly while in San Miguel de Allende. Mom had suffered from a hernia for many years, which she had ignored. She needed to go to the hospital and get surgery immediately. Amy got a call late one night, and she and I flew down right away. When we arrived at the hospital early the following morning, it was not like any hospital we had ever seen. Inside, it was dark and empty and quiet as a monastery. It had the eerie and serene ambiance of a painting from the Middle Ages. Instead of the bright lights and frantic pace you'd expect, there was nothing but darkness and silence. We walked tepidly down the hallway finding nobody at all, no patients, not even staff. We didn't see a single soul. But then we heard the echo of Mom's voice coming from a room at the end of the corridor. It sounded like she was giggling. A nurse appeared in nun's clothing, like a specter, and gestured us into the room.

Mom was indeed laughing. She was sat up in her bed, talking on the telephone and she looked happy as ever. What a relief to find her in good spirits. All night long, we had feared the worst. Like in many old Mexican buildings, the walls were thick and shadowy with almost no windows, and it was cool as a tomb. The doctor who had performed the surgery suddenly showed up, but he wasn't dressed like a doctor. He told us Mom would recover quickly and be out of the hospital in a day or two. He was also an important businessman in town, and he promptly excused himself to attend to other obligations. There was such a religious sense of calmness and somberness in that place. It didn't seem real, and yet everything was fine. Like a miracle, the emergency was over.

The hospital bill for the surgery was so cheap it was laughable. Mom had no medical insurance in Mexico, but that didn't matter. Nobody complained. We paid the bill without any fuss. Once again, the good karma of Mexico had protected her. The scare was over and we checked Mom out of the hospital two days later. Amy and I returned to the States by plane and Mom stayed in San Miguel for a short while longer. She visited with friends for a few more days and rested up. When she felt good enough to drive, she pulled herself back into the driver's seat and resumed her travels. She drove down to Guayabitos as usual to spend another month in Mexico.

A couple of weeks later, we received another emergency call. It was the hotel keeper, Jorge, who told Amy that Mom had suddenly been admitted to the hospital in Puerto Vallarta, which was about an hour from Guayabitos. She had a serious infection. Amy flew down again immediately and got Mom on a plane back to Los Angeles that same day. The two arrived in Santa Barbara late that night and Mom was checked into the hospital. Her kidneys were bad, and she was unable to eat and digest food. Eventually, she was discharged, but she still had complaints and found eating to be very difficult. In the meanwhile, the VW remained in Guayabitos. Jorge had parked the car in the hotel yard in the corner and covered it with palm fronds and other vegetation to keep it safely out of view. He was frequently out of town. Peggy knew she could count on Jorge to not let anything happen to the van, but it was going to be stuck down there for who knows how long, fifteen hundred miles away, hidden under the Mexican jungle, like an ancient Mayan ruin.

Back in Santa Barbara, Amy and I worried about Mom. She was living by herself now in the mobile home. She insisted that she was fine and didn't need any help. The doctors weren't sure what was wrong with her exactly. They gave her medication and continued to keep an eye on her. For the first time in decades, she was without her car, which made her more miserable than anything else. She was frustrated and restless. Without the van, she didn't know what to do with herself. She didn't have the mobility and freedom she was accustomed to.

Finally, after an intolerable month of inaction, she convinced Amy to fly her back to Mexico to pick up the car. That was the last thing Amy wanted to do, but she gave in to Mom's demands. They flew back down to Puerto Vallarta and rented a car up to Guayabitos where they found the van hidden under all the camouflage. It looked helpless and dispirited, like any old car abandoned in a junk yard, never to be driven again. It was the only time in decades that it had ever been ignored and not used. They pulled the van out of the weeds and cleaned her off. She needed a little mechanical reviving, and a good bath and some TLC, but she was going to be okay. Mom was going to be okay too. They both had a few good years left in them, and it was time to hit the road once more and do what they had always done.

Neither me nor Amy's husband was able to go down there at the time. Amy insisted that Mom not make the drive home on her own. Her only option was to go with her. Amy didn't have any experience driving the VW. She was used to new cars that were automatic and performed much better. She was skeptical and worried about the road conditions and the long hours of driving. In her eyes, it was absolutely crazy to drive so far in such an old car in a foreign and unknown country. Fortunately, it was not foreign or unknown from Peggy's perspective; she had made the trip dozens of times. She convinced Amy she could do it with her eyes closed. Finally, Amy relented and agreed to accompany her.

As it turned out, Mom ended up driving most of the way. She insisted on pushing on at the regular pace, even faster. The first day was ten hours of driving with barely a stop. Amy wanted to get home quickly too, but she could see that her mother was pushing herself to the brink. But Mom wasn't crazy; she was just driven as always. From years and years of experience, she knew what the van and her were capable of, and she insisted on completing the trip. They made it safely to the Belmar in Mazatlan and took a short rest. From there, they continued back up the normal route through Navojoa to Nogales and Yuma and made it back to Santa Barbara in four days. Amy said, "Never again!" Never again for her, anyway. But Mom got herself back into shape and continued to make the round-trip every year for the next five seasons. She kept visiting Julie in Canada, too.

Mom's health problems remained something that she mostly kept to herself, and from all outward appearances they did not seem to limit her. For Peggy, denial was the best medicine. Amy worried constantly, but I said you've got to let her do what she's got to do. That's her life. That's who she is. Looking back, I'm glad she never quit. I'm proud of her fortitude and her grit. Sooner or later it will be time for her to go, and she'll drive into the sunset doing what she loved—and being the soul that she was meant to be.

Chapter 17

The Six Million Dollar Van

In the forty-four years Peggy drove her VW, another car never charmed or seduced her or even caught her eye. She and Dad never bought another car or a second car. She stood by her van. It was like a marriage—the old-fashioned kind. People typically get rid of their cars before long. They don't look at them as an investment, because they aren't. Most cars depreciate and eventually become a liability. We kick them to the curb and say, "Good riddance. Time for a new one." It's a good thing we don't treat people that way. Right. If somebody traded in their aging dog or cat for a fluffy new one, we'd think they were cruel. But with cars it is expected, and replacing the old heap is seldom anything less than an occasion for celebration. They don't care about us, so why should we care about them? Peggy felt differently. Her loyalty to her van was genuine and steadfast. She believed that people would let you down. They'll betray and disappoint you ultimately, and unlike cars, their defects cannot be fixed, their broken parts cannot be replaced. It's very possible that deep inside, Peggy's heart was calloused against most humans. Not all. Julie could never betray her or disappoint her—not on purpose—but she couldn't be fixed either. You had no choice but to love such a person, as there was never an ego to contend with or to challenge your own ego. You would never want to hurt them or neglect them. Psychologically, Peggy may have understood that the only humans you can trust are the feeble-minded, because they are usually the only ones who are truly innocent and selfless. Everybody starts out like that, like a brand-new car, but at the first signs of any trouble, we are less forgiving, less patient, less loving, and less loyal towards them. It might be unconscious. No one wants to admit it.

A car can always be fixed. With patience and love and understanding, its faults can be worked out. It can be tinkered with, reconfigured, improved, and made whole. In essence, it can be cured, which makes it something that ultimately you can depend on forever. People, on the other hand, are shit. To think that the van could ever speak, obviously, is utter delusion. That it might thank you for an oil change or new brakes or a fancy coat of paint is nonsense. But like you pet a horse on the neck to show your appreciation for all that it does, a vehicle's owner rewards her car too, and it's nice to think at least that the car reciprocates that love. We don't take the time and money to dutifully and meticulously wash and detail our car just so it will look better; we do it because we know the car itself will feel better and be "happier." The happier it is, the more you spoil it and pamper it, the better it will perform. And if you ever curse it—watch out! How many times did the VW get that pep talk as it huffed and puffed up a steep grade? "Come on, you can do it. I believe in you. Don't let me down now, in my hour of need." There were times when the van was simply too exhausted to make it over the hill, but Peggy didn't take it personally. It could never ever let her down. It was not the car's fault. She had to treat it better next time. She simply knew that it was capable of so much greatness—more than the car itself even recognized. We are all much stronger than we believe we are. You have to dig deep within to find what you are truly capable of. It will be worth it. It will be liberating and joyous, the moment you finally realize the great potential you have inside you.

There is a dark chapter in this story. Not an evil darkness or a malicious darkness, but a secret darkness, a side that has been hidden. How it happened, nobody knows. It may have been neglect, absent-mindedness, or laziness on Peggy's part. It's hard to believe that it was any of these, considering the level of devotion and love Peggy had for her van. It was one of the anomalies that went bump in the night. It was a nightmare and a tragedy. Fortunately, in the end there was redemption and rebirth, love and forgiveness, salvation and eternal life.

Peggy was up in Canada to see Julie. She was visiting some friends there one night, and she parked the van on a hill in front of their house. She stayed very late and ended up spending the night. That is her side of the story and there is no reason to question it, other than the fact that eighty-year-old women don't normally crash on their friend's couch after partying all night. She did however sound a little guilty when she described the incident to Amy and me. However, there were no witnesses to contradict her statements, no investigation or police report. She had never had an accident in sixty years of driving, and the van had remained unscathed all its life. But when Peggy awoke the following morning, she found that the car was not parked in front of the house where she had left it. At the bottom of the hill, about a block away, she saw it. It was an inextricably crunched-up heap of metal, lodged against a solid cement wall. There it lay at the end of the street, fifty yards away. How that happened exactly has remained a dark mystery to this day. Peggy thought someone must have broken into the vehicle and tried to steal it, couldn't start it, and it had rolled backwards and crashed into the wall. That is entirely possible. All that is known is that the van was in horrific and irreparable shape. The word "shape" doesn't even apply; it was in pieces.

After Mom's death, I found a series of photographs of the car after the wreck. The pictures looked so bad that I gasped aloud. They showed the remains of a vehicle that had not just rolled backwards into a wall, but that looked like it had been pushed off a cliff! The photos were so ghastly that I immediately ripped them up. It looked like somebody had taken a sledgehammer and whacked the poor vehicle to a pulp. Right after the incident happened, Peggy called us in California to tell us the news. Other than the suspicious tinge in her voice, she did not sound forlorn or discouraged. She had gone to see the AAA agent. The vehicle had full collision insurance and they'd pay out a cash settlement. That should have been the end of a long and memorable life, and an admirable one at that. With the ten thousand dollars, she could have found a replacement. However, Peggy was not willing to just give up so easily. She insisted on a larger amount. It wasn't her character to take bad news without a fight. She was going to do whatever it took to save her baby.

Although the damage was to the rear and side of the car, the engine was relatively unharmed. As was her nature, she started persistently seeking out and visiting various mechanics and au-to-body repair shops. The engine was salvageable, but the fenders were impossible to repair. Her only hope was to find an identical VW in a junk yard somewhere that had the body parts needed. The chances of finding one that matched the make and model, and which was still in good condition was practically impossible. Better to just take the loss and move on. But not Peggy. Once again, the clouds parted, God shone down his omnipotent light, and a miracle occurred.

She called every junk yard in the area, from Victoria to Seattle to Portland, and every mechanic and body shop in between. Within a few short weeks, she heard back from a junk yard who said they might have what she was looking for. Lo and behold, it turned out they had a VW that was an identical match. She refused the insurance company's offer and told them she was opting to repair the vehicle. Everyone shook their heads. Like Humpty-Dumpty, they put the car back together again. It was like the Six Million Dollar Van. The engine had to be removed and reinstalled, which was easy enough. The second fenders fit like the seamless tiles of a jigsaw puzzle and the car's rear section was completely restored. Finding the right color paint was the next challenge. The van had last been painted an original shade of mocha that Peggy had carefully chosen. The repair shop found a blend that matched the color almost perfectly. Upon close examination, an expert could barely detect the difference, but it was so close the average layman would never notice. To this day, it remains unchanged.

"All's well that ends well" was what Ron always used to say. Peggy got on the road again and made the drive back to California as if nothing had happened. She was very proud to show off the fine work. Her mechanics in Santa Barbara were speechless. Not only could they not believe that she was able to locate a forty-year-old fender from the graveyards of history, but that she had been persistent and unrelenting enough to carry out the task. She never lost faith, never doubted, and never quit. She brought up the story occasionally, but unless you had seen the damage yourself or the photos, you'd never realize how the van had ever survived certain death. It had literally been in the clutches of hell—and it had returned and been redeemed.

After that, Peggy went along as though nothing ever fazed or interrupted her. Together, she and her van were indestructible. She knew it. The same trips continued for the next several years, and people who knew her and recognized the van continued to wave and watch her drive by. Never give up. You won't regret it. As the famous adage goes: It's not over until the fat lady sings, and Peggy was no opera star.

Chapter 18

Answers

It became more and more obvious, as Mom got older, that her eternally restless spirit had its roots in her childhood. Just a year or two before her death, she decided she was going to find out the truth about her adoption. The facts she knew were that she had been born in New York City in 1930, and that her real mother (and father) had given her up for reasons that most likely were the result of financial hardship. It was the beginning of the Great Depression, after all. But she had been saved from all that and was adopted by a couple who had the means to raise her comfortably.

After the war and graduating from high school, she was fortunate enough to be able to attend a good college and to graduate with a master's degree. Obviously, her parents made this possible. She had focus and drive, and definitely possessed the intelligence and skills to make her own way in the world. She was fiercely independent and ambitious compared to a lot of women her age who were more content to settle into traditional matrimony during prosperous times. She remained single, traveled throughout Europe, worked as a home economics teacher, until the age of 34, when she met her husband and had a family.

Now she was 84 and she wanted to know finally about her real parents. Unfortunately, she got distracted in this pursuit temporarily by some spectacular headlines in the news that took her deep into her own unknown history. Huguette Clark was an heiress and a recluse who had recently died at the age of 104. She owned a giant mansion on a hill overlooking the Pacific in Santa Barbara. It was one of many houses Huguette owned that she had never visited. It was elegantly maintained year after year, and had a full staff of servants ready around the clock for her arrival, but she never stayed there once. The heiress was the daughter of a Midwest senator and copper tycoon, who had left her an inexhaustible fortune. She had an enormous doll collection and the biggest apartment in Manhattan. Huguette Clark's life story appeared in the local papers and was suddenly gaining a lot of attention. All her life, she had lived in opulence as a recluse. Huguette had had a very brief marriage, which according to her biographers, was never "consummated." The heartbroken young heiress spent the rest of her long and lonely life secluded in a lavish penthouse. She had no siblings or children, and now the lawyers and any and all distant relatives were fighting for a piece of the massive estate.

Mom started having unrealistic fantasies about her birth mother. She convinced herself that she was the illegitimate daughter of the heiress. As the details of Huguette's intriguing story began to dominate the local newspapers, Mom was beginning to dig into the mystery of her own past. She started connecting the dots: Huguette's date of birth, where she had lived, the date of her suddenly ended marriage, photos of her, and other curious facts and trivia. Mom finally came to the conclusion that she was very likely the long-lost daughter of the heiress. That sounds far-fetched and it was. There was however a very uncanny resemblance in at least one old photo between the two women when they were young.

It was pretty apparent at this point that Mom was desperately seeking some kind of closure in her life. She had always been intensely driven to find answers, to make sense of the big picture of her life and her motivations for being who she was and living the way she had. It was interesting. She definitely wasn't suffering from dementia; she was as sharp as ever mentally. She was however experiencing a mild bout of delusion, and who could blame her? She wanted the truth finally, and why shouldn't the truth be fantastical?

Her adoption records had been permanently sealed, as per the law in the state of New York. Her adopted mother had known the details about her birth parents but had refused to share them with Peggy as a teenager. Her mother ended up burning those records in a jealous fit of anger. That was probably what motivated Peggy to leave home as a young woman and never want to look back. After that, she had a contentious and unpleasant relationship with her mother and only resentfully fulfilled her obligations as her daughter. Her mother had become a grouchy drinker after the death of her husband. Mom had no brothers or sisters either.

Like most of us, Peggy was always trying to prove something she probably didn't understand fully. Through the tenaciousness that had always characterized her, she was eventually successful in convincing the adoption agency that at her age, her parents were obviously deceased by now. Finally, the agency agreed to open her file and disclose the records and the details of her adoption. That provided the truth finally, or parts of it, and she was able to face the fact that she wasn't the long-lost daughter of who she thought she was.

Mom was always a very practical and skeptical individual. When the Huguette fantasy briefly took her over, I saw a vulnerable and hurt child in her coming to the surface. For a short while, she was acting like a kind of naive and entitled little girl, which was the exact opposite of who she had always been. Maybe it would have been a happier ending for her if she had died believing a fantasy, but I truly felt she wanted to leave this earth with her feet and her wheels still on the ground. Like she had always been with me, I thought I had an obligation to be frank with her. It was not that I took any pleasure in confronting her; it was very hard for me to do, but I think I owed her so much.

I told her, "You know, Mom...I understand how being adopted must leave a person with a terrible feeling about why it happened. They must feel like it was their fault, they weren't good enough. But the truth is that your parents had nothing. Literally, they could have been starving. Don't assume they were living it up and being selfish and irresponsible. It was the Depression, and your Mom was too young. She was just a kid. I'm sure she didn't want to do it. We know she tried for months to take care of you. She must have felt utterly hopeless and she must have felt terribly guilty too. I know it's hard but try to give her a break. What would you have done in that situation? Try to really see that. It wasn't your fault."

She had obviously thought about all this before, but it hadn't given her much consolation. It was an emotional burden that had built up over the years.

"Who knows?" she said.

Then came the hard part. I said, "I'm sure it is a common kind of...fantasy...to want to believe that one day your parents will return, and they will explain that it was all a big mix-up, and then you will be reunited, and you'll live happily ever after in a castle of gold."

She chuckled ironically.

"What's the alternative?" I said. "That they were cruel and careless people who threw out a child, like garbage into the streets? Sorry - but you know what I mean. It's normal to feel the way you do. But it wasn't your fault, Mom."

I had never talked to her like that before. It was very personal and uncomfortable for both of us. I thought it would only be more harmful in the long run if she kept up with this Huguette Clark thing. I didn't want to hurt her, but the fantasies were turning her into a person I didn't recognize. There were signs that she was reverting to a helpless child, and I just couldn't accept her that way. She had a right to believe whatever she wanted, but she had always been so strong and practical about the world, and I couldn't let it happen.

Fortunately, I watched her gradually snap out of it. In the end, it wasn't because of me, but because of the real facts she was finally getting. She read and studied all the documents that were available. She read letters from the records that explained what she never knew, and which provided the closure she genuinely needed. It was not a story dreamed-up for self-protection, a lie to console her in her final years; it was the truth, and that is what she had always strived for and insisted on. She didn't escape into nostalgia like most people do. She finished up strong and remained as clear-headed and realistic about life as she had always been. It was pointless to speculate or worry about the things she couldn't control. She couldn't rewrite the past. It was a hard pill to swallow, but she more than anybody had what it took.

Mom seemed to be able to finally understand and forgive a certain element of humanity, those people or forces she believed had wronged her. For most of her life, she seemed to have had little tolerance for complainers. That attitude may have often come across as quite cold and unfeeling. The lesson, however, was that you should never feel sorry for yourself. To hell with everybody else. Pull yourself up by your own bootstraps and don't take any crap from anybody! In her final years, she softened up considerably. She wasn't so tough on others or with herself. She became a very nice old lady, which is always the best way to finish up.

Chapter 19
Big Mamma

Peggy was always in pursuit of a rich life. To have a truly rich life requires just enough money, not too much. You want to have what you need, but not much more than that. The most important thing you can possess is ownership of yourself, to know who you are and to stick to your values and principles, to determine and decide your own future.

She taught home economics to kids for most of her career. After retiring, she volunteered at a school in San Miguel de Allende that was an orphanage more or less for disadvantaged children who had no family or other means of support. But she didn't live for her work. She lived for herself, and when there was a holiday or time off, she wanted to use that time to go out and see things and places and people and fill her life with experiences that really meant something. She was dependent on no one, and didn't like following the crowd or doing what other people expected. She thought most people were too influenced by others. They ended up conforming and making compromises and not being true to themselves. They didn't go after what they wanted and what they believed they deserved. You don't always get what you want, but you should always appreciate what you have and use it. In many ways, she was selfish—but nobody's perfect.

There eventually came a time, although it never was obvious to her, that she didn't need to keep pushing and pushing on so hard. Amy tried to make her see this. "You should settle down, Mom. We worry about you taking these long trips by yourself. What if something happened to you? You should get rid of the van. It's old. It's a liability. It could break down. Why spend so much money fixing it, when you could buy a new car, a better car, a more economical car, a more stylish car?"

Peggy thought about it. "Maybe you're right," she said. "But not now. I've come this far, and I'm not finished yet. There's a little more I want to do and see, a few more things on my list. Not yet." She smiled briefly, and for just a moment showed signs of genuine contentment and satisfaction. "Maybe when I'm in heaven—or wherever I end up...I'll have a snazzy little sports car. A zippy one, and I can whiz around the clouds like a bird. That sounds fun. We'll see."

But Peggy didn't really believe in heaven. It was never her intention to live in a dream world—not on purpose. Hadn't she just been sucked into all that nonsense? Yes, life was easier now, but that's not the point. She'd look out the window and see the van there, waiting for her. It was always encouraging her, and always ready to go. It was never too tired, too lazy, too indifferent, or apathetic. *Why should I be that way either?* Peggy thought. What good is a car that doesn't move, and what good is a person who stays in a rocking chair? I'll never be like that!

She slowly pulled her stiff and heavy body off the sofa, determined to keep moving, to get out of the house and do the things that she needed to do. She had to go to the post office, and to the linen store, and to take that chair in with the wobbly leg, to have the furniture repairman look at it. She had to visit the bank manager and get new checks, get that zipper repaired on her windbreaker, and pick up a jar of cocktail onions, or stop by and see Betty Johnson. There was always something to do and somewhere to go, and the littlest errands seemed to take up more and more energy, but that didn't stop her. At some point, there would be no more things left to do or time to do them. Then what? It was something she didn't want to think about, something to deny and postpone. There must be an end to the road. But not now.

I came to live with Mom in the final months before she passed away. She had to spend three weeks in a convalescent hospital, then came home for a while, and was in and out of the main hospital for a few days on a number of occasions. Eventually, she could no longer pull herself up to stand, and we got her a wheelchair. It was a sad day when she stopped driving altogether. She had commanded that vehicle of hers with power and determination for forty-four years, taking the wheel by the horns, and pushing the pedal to the metal. How many millions of times had she shifted the gears and tapped the brakes, checked the mirrors, and turned the key?

Amy and I brought her back from the convalescent home. She took the keys out of her purse and handed them to me. That was the last time. Actually, there was only a single key. It fit all the doors and the ignition. The stories that key could tell, all the memories, all the situations, all the worlds it had opened up, and the dreams it had unlocked. Hoisting Mom up to get her onto the front seat of the van was impossible. We opened the car's sliding door and carefully maneuvered her out of her wheelchair. She had to sit on the floor in the back of the van. Imagine how she felt being hauled home like that, like some heavy and burdensome load. It was one of the few times that she had ever been a passenger. She resigned herself to the reality that she was no longer in charge. On the freeway, driving her home, I heard her yell from the back, "Alan, is the car in fourth gear? It sounds like it's not in fourth gear." She was right, but after that she stopped giving orders. A few days later, I told her I must have accidently left the radio on, and the car wouldn't start. She responded indifferently, "That's okay." I looked at her, she didn't care anymore. That's when I knew she would never drive the van again. In the past that never would have been okay; that would have been the cause for a stern lecture. She never mentioned the car again. She didn't ask how it was, if it was running fine. Within a couple short weeks her own battery was drained, and that was the end.

Mom passed away on Mother's Day, 2016. She had lived a full life of eighty-six years. We had taken her to the hospital one last time. Everybody was around her and she seemed happy about all the attention. The nurse confided to us that Mom was probably going to die the next day. We decided we should tell her, and she looked absolutely shocked. She didn't understand what was wrong, why they couldn't figure it out, or fix her. She kept saying, "They're going to find out there is nothing wrong with me. You'll see. It's a big mistake." But then everything stopped working, and it was all over.

In the months following her death, I spent the summer cleaning out the house and the car. There was a lot of old stuff stashed inside the van, but it wasn't messy. It had been eight years since Ron had died, and she had not used the back cabin of the car for much, except to transport things or to drive friends or family around once in a while. She had not done any camping without Dad, or used the supplies that were stored in the various shelves and compartments. The pop-up top had been ignored for years. Overall, everything still looked in good shape. I spent several days pulling out stuff from under and behind the seats and in the cabinets and other spots. I found all the tools and camping supplies and the silverware and plastic plates that had been in there and unused for years.

The car was mine now. I decided to re-organize everything to suit me. I didn't change much. I made sure whatever I kept worked and was useful. There was a good chance that the house would sell quickly and that I might have to temporarily make the van my home. That actually felt consoling. I had the summer off, and the idea of going camping and traveling around was a way to reconnect with the old memories and to Mom and to Dad. There would be plenty of room to make it my own personal man cave on wheels, compared to the days when the whole family filled it up. It was a project I worked on all summer. I got to where it was really nice. There was even room for my bicycle now, and my guitar. I got really excited. I felt more at home in the van than I felt anywhere. I vowed to drive it forever and carry on the tradition and Mom's legacy. Whatever repairs it needed it would get. She was mine now and I'd take care of her. I gave her the nickname: "Big Mamma."

Everywhere I went, people commented on the van and asked me questions about it. People offered to buy it on the spot. I experienced a feeling of great pride and contentment. I trusted the car to not let me down. That feeling of trust and loyalty was built upon all the memories I had, all the long trips and the short ones, all the conversations and arguments and stories, all the years, the good times and the tough times. They all came flooding back. They surrounded me and nurtured me. I remembered my father sitting at the helm, the gestures and the expressions he made, humming as he drove. I remembered the determination with which Mom manhandled the steering wheel, how she constantly checked the mirrors and looked over her shoulder. Those actions were all a part of me too: the sound of the heavy door sliding open and shut, the smell and the texture of the seats, the touch of the knobs on the radio and the dashboard, the sound of the antenna bouncing in the wind. There were decades of emotions echoing the past. I'd compare it to when you visit your grandmother's house: old-fashioned and a little spooky, but familiar—it was a home. Best of all, grandma's house had wheels. I could take it wherever I went and wherever I wanted. And despite its age, the car didn't act old at all. It wasn't any slower. It wasn't taking medication for high oil pressure. Its bumpers weren't receding, and its headlights hadn't dimmed over the years. Its joints didn't creak or suffer from the ravages of car-thritis. It still had the pep and vigor of a teenager. Frankly, it was in better shape than I was. Mom always maintained the car and never let it fall into decline. She took it to the mechanic every three thousand miles and gave it whatever it needed. I think that's why she was in such denial when her own time finally came, and Dad's time too. She couldn't get it in her head that something couldn't be fixed. It was unacceptable to her. It was illogical. It was nonsense. I decided that her soul had never quit. Now her soul occupied the van, and she would go on forever—like she always had.

Chapter 20
Get Off Your Butt!

The Mexicans have a funny slang expression: *Huevon.* It literally means "big egg" or "giant eggs," and refers to a man's testicles. You see, if a man's eggs are too big and too heavy, he is unable to get up off the sofa and work. Such a man is not macho, he's lazy, and huevon is definitely an insult. In the summer of 2020, I was huevon. The country was in lockdown. The world had come to a halt, and I was spending my days doing absolutely nothing. I was having dreams about Mom. She was on my case, urging me to get off my butt and do something. The dreams started getting more frequent and more pressing. I was sleeping too much, which was causing me to have nightmares. I was escaping. I wasn't living my life the way I should. I wasn't living at all. It was a restlessness that I was denying and avoiding. Let's face it, it was fear.

Mom had been gone for four years. When she passed away, there was never any question that I would keep the van. But for what? Either it was purely for sentimental reasons, or it was something else. I knew what that something else was, but I was afraid to do it. I had a great opportunity before me. Mom kept telling me so. It got to the point where I couldn't deny it anymore. I looked out my front window and saw the van looking back at me. I didn't have any excuses left.

I remembered when I was young, how we couldn't wait for summer. Every kid feels the same, but if there's no plan, they quickly get bored. Mom never wasted a second; she always knew where we were going, even if the rest of us had no idea. We needed her and we trusted her to make the plans and prepare for the trips. As soon as we were out of school, the very next day, we were all loaded in the van and on our way to a brand-new place. Now, in my dreams, she was just a ghost, an invisible spirit without a body, without a vehicle any longer to explore this earthly sphere. She was telling me to make the most of what I had. Don't let it go to waste. Finally, I got to the point where I had to face what I was afraid of and do what needed to be done.

Even though I kept it and had no other car, I was hardly driving the van at all. A couple years earlier, I had returned to San Miguel de Allende. I spent two months there enjoying the town that I loved and remembered so well. But I left the VW in a garage in California. She never should have forgiven me. I didn't want anything to happen to the car, but it was cowardly to leave her like that. It was a sin. Now I was just protecting it for posterity, like china in a cabinet. The mechanic told me I'd need new tires soon. It wasn't from the miles; they were just getting old. I could hear Mom's voice. She was pissed. "Tires rotting from not being used? You should be ashamed." She was right. The whole point of a car is to drive it, and the point of the camper was to go camping and traveling and seeing all there is to see. I was pampering it and protecting it from the world, but in doing so, I was putting it out to pasture. What's worse, I was putting myself out to pasture. What the hell was I waiting for? The Second Coming? Was I going to ride Jesus around in the van, like a golden chariot, when He finally came back? It was a waste. I was letting Mom down, too.

I took the unemployment money and bought a set of brand-new tires, and I told the mechanics to give the car whatever she needed to prepare for a big trip. Mom had a good relationship with the guys at the shop. She had been going to the same place for years, and they knew she had driven on long hauls to Canada and Mexico regularly. They said the motor was in great shape and ready for anything. I told them I had a friend in New Mexico who I wanted to visit. His house was at seven or eight thousand feet. I'd be going through the desert and climbing some big mountains. They said, "Go for it," but I was still chicken. I just didn't possess the same confidence they had, or that Mom had always had. Why was I thinking so negatively? I realized I was being selfish, only thinking about my own security. That's not the way I was raised. That's not Peggy's son. Most of all, that is not what the van wants, what it loves to do. It was time to become the man of the family.

We would do it together. I made up my mind. Sure, I was scared. That's the point. That was the whole damn point.

The dreams went away, but now I could hear the van talking to me. It was Mom speaking to me through the van. It was like a pep talk from a mentor. She was saying, "Let's go out and have some fun. I won't let you down. C'mon, let's do it!" It sounds odd to believe a car has that kind of life and soul inside of it; that it has the ability to communicate and to inspire, and to give you that warm feeling only the best of friends can provide. To believe that takes a lot of imagination. It takes an unusual kind of faith. It takes faith in a machine that is fifty years old, but still has a life and a purpose and an inner need to perform, to keep going—not only for its own sake, but for the good of those close to it, to its family. Never has a car existed like this one. It is a car who doesn't want to give up and who doesn't want you to give up either. I know that is hard to believe, but it's true.

Chapter 21

Travels with Charlie

I left on the second of June and picked Charlie up in Las Vegas. As soon as I arrived, the temperature shot up to l07 degrees. We waited for a few days for it to cool off, and then headed for New Mexico. Outside of Mesquite, we stopped for gas, and the car didn't start. Not a click, not a sound. That had never happened to me before. It must be too hot. We waited a half hour and she started. Thank God. The rest of the way, we always kept the engine running whenever we refueled. Charlie said that if we encountered a mountain we couldn't make it over, we'd just have to take a break, and do it in sections. He'd covered the territory dozens and dozens of times, and he was like Mom, never with any fear or hesitation about not making it. He told me he had driven the entire thousand miles from California to New Mexico without stopping. It took him eighteen hours, he said, and he had done it more than once. Charlie knew where the gas stations were, the motels, the best places to stock up on food and beer. I told him we had to get gas again soon. The gauge had always been a little shaky and inaccurate, so I kept my eye on the miles and wrote everything down, as Mom had. She said to fill up every two hundred miles. Now we were at 209 and I was worried. Mom told me that once she had made it to 230. I asked Charlie how much farther to the next gas station and he said, forty miles or so. Hell! The car had never run out of gas in its whole life. Charlie seemed so cavalier, and I was such a baby—but he was just joking when he said forty miles, and we made it.

I know Charlie wanted to go a lot faster, but he was patient and let me do all the driving. We went through the colorful desert at Lake Powell and the Navajo Nation, and briefly through Utah. We weaved back and forth through two or three states. We stayed in

Kanab the first night and the second night we were in Cortez. We stopped for lunch at the mining town of Durango. He showed me where the train went through the mountain and he knew all about the history. It gave me a lot of confidence to make that trip with Charlie, to have him as a guide and a companion. We got to his house near Chama on the third day and I stayed there for a week.

I started thinking about what I was going to do next. We had been lucky to escape some very hot days. If I turned around and went back the same way we had come, it would be too hot. I announced to him that I was going to keep going. I was going to head north to Colorado, Wyoming, Mt. Rushmore, South Dakota, and try to make it to North Dakota. From there I'd turn around and come back through Montana, Yellowstone, Idaho, and Oregon. Except for Oregon, these were states I had never been to. My parents had been to all those places in the van already. They had visited Yellowstone and Mt. Rushmore without us kids. They had driven to Ottawa and dipped down to visit Michigan, Minnesota, Wisconsin, and Iowa. I had asked my mother once if there were any states they hadn't been to. She said they had never gone to North Dakota, so that's where I aimed for. I decided to just go for it.

The day I left, it was Charlie's birthday. I told him that I was going to head north and try to make it to Pueblo next. He pointed me in the right direction. I would have to climb over Cumbres Pass, not far from where we were in northern New Mexico. That was a ten-thousand-foot mountain. By now, I had the confidence to face that challenge. He told me how beautiful it would be. He was right; it was amazing country. Near the peak it got pretty cold. The road curved quite a bit and I spent a lot of time downshifting into third gear, but there was no traffic and no trucks and I had the mountain to myself. I was very proud of the van. I came down the other side in no time, entered the Colorado desert and it was hot again. I made it to Pueblo in the early afternoon and parked the van for a rest on the outskirts of town. I waited an hour, but the van didn't start. This time I didn't panic. I was prepared for what to expect. I had everything I needed, including plenty of time. I was next to a city park with a public restroom, and I could stay there overnight if I needed. I took my bike out of the car and cruised around the neighborhood. There was a Mexican restaurant and a liquor store. It was very hot. I tried to start her again. Nothing. All I could do was wait it out and hope she started when it got cooler in the evening. The worst case was that I'd have to hop on my bike again and go find a mechanic, but I held tight and took a nap in the van. I was in the shade at least, and I had a phone. My parents never had a phone. I'd be okay.

I woke up a couple hours later and tried her one more time. She started right up and was purring like a kitty cat. I threw my bike in the car and headed for the town center to find a hotel. By nightfall it started to rain a little. From then on, I decided to always head straight for the center of town. Every town had an old historic district where I could park the van, pull out my bike and cruise around and check everything out. I could find a suitable motel without having to turn the engine on and off. That plan worked great everywhere I went. I got to see a lot on my bike and learned where things were without having to drive up and down.

I had seriously considered leaving my bicycle at home. It was an old beach cruiser and pretty heavy, but it ended up being an invaluable asset. It just barely fit inside the car's back cabin; one inch bigger and it wouldn't have fit. When I slept in the car, I took the bike out and locked it up next to the van. The coolest part was riding around on a beach cruiser in places like Wyoming and Montana. If my friends in Santa Barbara could see me now! It was one more of those comforts of home that I had along with me that made all the difference. I'm glad I brought my guitar too. There were places where there was no Internet, and I passed the night playing songs and drinking beer. I opened the sliding door and hung out on the porch all night singing at the moon and enjoying the summer nights. I had everything I needed. It was perfect.

Every night I studied the elevations of the towns I was headed for. I was fortunate that I never encountered any extreme climbs or descents. I got lucky, I guess. I eventually discovered that for a good part of my trip, I was following the old Oregon Trail of the pioneers who also avoided the steepest grades and tried to follow the path of least resistance. But I didn't purposely do that; I just had good luck—and I had a good car. Day after day, the van took it in stride and I got where I needed to go. I also made a daily check of the next day's temperatures. It was the middle of June, and it was regularly in the upper eighties and nineties. I had two choices. Either I got up at the break of dawn and completed a couple hundred miles before it was too hot, or I spent another day in town and waited for it to cool off. I had no A/C and only an air-cooled engine, so I always had to monitor the motor's heat. My parents had an extra gauge installed for that purpose. From Pueblo, I went to Boulder, then Cheyenne, Casper, Rapid City, Pierre, Bismark, Miles City, Billings, Bozeman, Yellowstone, Idaho Falls, Twin Falls, Burns, Bend, Eugene, Bandon, Willis, Santa Cruz, and finally Santa Barbara. I came back to town from the opposite direction as I had left. The whole loop took thirty-two days.

There were many things I wanted to ask Mom about the car, but it was too late. For example, in the strong wind, was it normal for the van to get pushed around so much? Charlie and I had been bullied from lane to lane in the desert through the Four-Corners area. It was scary. I figured it was the boxy shape of the van, and we just had to deal with it. I had to learn from my own experience all over again. At least I knew that if they had made it, so would I. Whatever they had been through, and whatever the van had come up against was nothing new. That's what I kept saying to myself: "The van has seen it all, and it has always survived." Even though I wrote down all the mileage and the prices for gas along the way, I wasn't keeping track of how far I had gone. I didn't want to jinx myself. It wasn't until I arrived back in Santa Barbara safely that I checked to see the total. I had driven 5,201 miles!

I drove for long distances where I saw no other cars at all. It was easier than I thought. The whole country had been shut down by a pandemic, and hardly anybody was traveling that summer. It felt free and open and timeless. The van never let me down. I didn't plan anything; I just drove to the next place, without any pressure, without a deadline, without anybody telling me where to go, or when to go, or how to go, or why to go. Mom was over my shoulder, prompting me, making her voice known, approving or cautioning me. It had all gone so smoothly, as she had promised.

At Mt. Rushmore, the forest ranger said the Black Hills were a place of sanctuary, to escape from the long hot summers and the shadeless plains. The Native Americans and the pioneers had sought out the hills "for rest." I drove to Pierre, South Dakota, along an endless road surrounded by beautiful green and yellow grass. It was like a giant golf course in every direction. There were slight hills that ever-so-gently rose and fell. There were no cars, no people, no animals, no activity. Occasionally, a town came up that wasn't a town at all, just a barn or two, with a few small houses. There was one sign, "Population: 39." A half an hour later, there was another place which had a population of only nine. They were towns named after a single man, like "Thomas," which made sense. If I broke down, they'd call it Vanville. and that is where I'd live out my days. That didn't happen. I crossed my fingers and kept driving.

I arrived at Pierre, and I suddenly saw the Missouri River. I didn't know it would be there. It sure looked nice. The girl working at the motel was admiring my van. She came out of the office and took pictures. She told me her dream was to buy a VW just like mine and tour around the country, but she said her parents wouldn't let her. They warned her that it wasn't safe, and the van could break down and leave her in the middle of nowhere. I told her I had made it all the way from California. I said, "Don't listen to them." It didn't help my case that there was a truck driver in the motel who had been stranded in Pierre for over a week. He was waiting for a part to be shipped out. It made me appreciate my good fortune. That's all you can do. Be thankful for your blessings and have empathy for other people who weren't so lucky this time.

He recommended the Mexican restaurant next to the motel. It was owned by a family from Guadalajara. The food really hit the spot. I talked to the owner and asked her if there were a lot of Mexicans in South Dakota. "Not really," she said. There certainly weren't any VW vans on the road. It was pretty cool being the only car with California plates. People honked enthusiastically when they passed. In the old days, they honked because we were too slow. They were friendly and hospitable everywhere I went, which put a smile on my face.

I pointed at my van out the window of the cafe, and I told the lady that it had been to Guadalajara many times. I remembered my parents visiting me there when I was in my twenties. They drove the van over to the neighborhood where I was living and took me for a ride. I showed them my school where I worked near the old center of the city and we went out for dinner. That seemed like yesterday. The first time we visited Guadalajara I was eight years old. My parents took us to the giant marketplace, where I saw red bananas for the first time. That was in 1972, when the van was new. I asked her if she missed Mexico, and she said, "Of course." I drank a Dos Equis and we chatted in Spanish.

It's a big world, but it's a small world too. Guadalajara seemed like the farthest place from Pierre, South Dakota—but here we were. You're never really separated, no matter how far the distance. It's the same ground beneath your feet. You just have to move your tires. Before you know it, you're in a different time and place. I could say to her, "Hop in the van. Let's go to Guadalajara!"—and we'd be there again, as far-fetched as it seems. You just have to do it, and it will happen, if you want.

After Pierre, I made my way to North Dakota. My final destination was Bismarck before turning back westward again. It was open and sunny driving, hot but not too hot. I passed my first vehicle since I had started. It was a tractor putt-putting down the road, even slower than I was going. But the van never felt too slow. It traveled at a very nice speed. North Dakota had no mountains and not many trees. In Wyoming, they were in the distance only. In Colorado, and later Montana and Oregon, the mountains were the steepest. I held my breath and pushed her as hard as I could. A little more... a little bit more... She never complained. She was never weak. I breathed again, and down we sailed like the wind.

Chapter 22

Home Again

The details of this trip, or any other, are nothing spectacular. Every traveler has his personal and unique experiences. For me, it was the small things, the feelings of a lone rider, on a horse, clopping along slowly, steadily, in the hot sun, from one town to the next, always eager to get there, realizing it's all the same long journey, a journey of the soul, a tiring journey, a fulfilling journey. That's what our lives are. We keep moving, we get there, and then we keep going. What else is there really, to being human? You move on, to pass the time, you listen, you watch, you wait. For what? Someday you'll know. Maybe. Someday it will all present itself. Then you will see. In the meantime, you keep moving, keep going, keep living.

From Bend, I shot over the pass at Mount Bachelor, and began the last big descent. After that, I felt I was back in my neck of the woods. I drove down through the Willamette Forest. It was the prettiest summer day, and there were bright flowers growing amidst the trees. It wasn't dark in the forest; it was as light as could be, the sun dancing off the leaves and illuminating everything there was to see. The air was fresh and bright. Birds were chirping happily. The wildlife was playing. I pulled over and got out of the car, taking it all in, appreciating the moment, that eternal moment. Today I would reach the Pacific Ocean—in a Volkswagen van. It's something anybody can do: to go for a trip in your car. You can use your car to accomplish the chores in life, or to go on a Sunday drive. You shouldn't neglect the Sunday drive, or else your life won't be any fun. It's not that hard, it's not a big deal. It's an opportunity you get, so take it.

I suddenly remembered how she had always been with me. From the time I was a young boy, she had taken me to a million

101

places. My lifelong companion and childhood friend. Now I was coming home again. I got inside and started the engine. What a gift, I thought. What a gift it is to be alive and in the world.

The Ballad of Big Mamma

She's a good car, Ma
You took us so very far
Now you drive a snazzy, little sports car
You're a good car, Ma

Driving from state to state
The world is hers to take
Nothing ever gonna stop or slow her down
She says the foolish hesitate
My life's too short to wait
So baby, let's move our wheels across the ground!

Climbing up over the Rockies
Take a left down to Mexico
Winding back up the coast through the Redwood trees
Somewhere inside she knows
She goes where the river flows
Being the soul that she was meant to be

She's a good car, Ma
You took us so very far
Now you drive a snazzy, little sports car
You're a good car, Ma

Cruising through the desert night
Steady as a bird in flight
Making her way out west to the open sea
Strong as the wind that blows
She follows the path she chose
Chasing the road of life - and being free

She's a good car, Ma
You took us so very far
Now you drive a snazzy, little sports car
You're a good car, Ma

About the Author

Alan Hurst was born in 1964. He is a teacher and a writer who resides in Santa Barbara, California. He drives a Volkswagen camper van, which his parents purchased in 1972.

Get in touch with him at alhurst@hotmail.com